JANET SCHAEFFLER, OP

prayer
FROM **A** TO **Z**

{ For catechists and those they teach }

TWENTY THIRD 23rd
PUBLICATIONS
www.23rdpublications.com

TWENTY-THIRD PUBLICATIONS
A Division of Bayard
One Montauk Avenue, Suite 200
New London, CT 06320
(860) 437-3012 or (800) 321-0411
www.23rdpublications.com

ISBN 978-1-58595-838-2
Library of Congress Catalog Card Number: 2011927377
Printed in the U.S.A.

CONTENTS

Introduction

Many years ago, I participated in a week-long retreat/workshop that centered on the Myers-Briggs Type Indicator and its relationship to spirituality and prayer. I didn't realize it until I arrived, but a friend of mine, a sister in my community, was attending also.

About halfway through the week, Jean said to me, "Janet, this is the most freeing thing I've ever experienced. I am so grateful."

When I asked her what she meant, she replied, "For the first forty years of my religious life, I thought I was a bad nun. Now, here this week, I realize that in those days (prior to the Second Vatican Council) — when we all prayed exactly the same way, and it never varied — we were praying in a way that was far from the preference of my personality type. I never had an opportunity to pray in those years with the forms and types of prayer which connected with, resonated with my personality type. After the Council, as we — like many others — began to rediscover the rich heritage of prayer within our tradition and retained our prayer forms of the past, but also added to them, I discovered all the vast and precious forms of prayer we have."

The conversation with Jean and especially her experience of not feeling worthy left an indelible memory with me. What an astounding, humbling responsibility we have.

Prayer is formative. Prayer is certainly and foremost our union with God, our openness to God, who loves us beyond words, more than we can even begin to wrap our minds around. Yet, prayer is also formative. Each and every time we pray, we are formed; something happens to us. We are changed; our perceptions change; who we are changes. Our prayer changes (and grows). Our relationship with God changes.

If we provide and surround our children, our youth, and our adults with only one kind of prayer experience (or only a few kinds), what is that teaching them about prayer? What is that teaching them about themselves? How is that forming their prayer lives? How is that forming their relationship with our extravagantly loving God?

What if the prayer experiences we provide—as good and meaningful as they are—are not the prayer forms that appeal to their personality types, their ways of learning, their ways of perceiving and responding in the world?

What an astounding, humbling responsibility we have. As Catholic Christians today, we are immersed in a rich, beautiful tradition of prayer. What a privilege it is to pass that on to all with whom we journey. Our children/youth (as well as their parents and all the adults we touch) will build their faith upon their prayer life—for the rest of their lives.

Our astounding and humbling responsibility challenges us to share with them as many of the prayer forms and methods as we can, so that they have many experiences and forms upon which to draw, so they can choose the ones that are most helpful for them in their growing, developing relationship with God.

This book is one help to support catechists in doing that. It certainly does *not* contain every prayer form, every method! But there are many (in alphabetical order). Numerous ones, of course, are going to appeal to you, and there are some that won't. Many will appeal to some of your young people and others won't, because of different personalities, different preferences in ways of responding, different ways of praying.

The beginning of each new section in the book — each letter — starts with a story or a quote (or both) followed by reflection questions — for you. Thus, this book isn't just ideas for catechetical methods and prayer experiences with our young pray-ers (as important as that is); it is also a chance for us to reflect on our prayer, as well as on our role as prayer leaders with our children/youth.

Before our alphabet of prayer ideas and methods, we begin with two reflections — which contain practical ideas — on our privileged roles as prayer leaders and as developers of a contemplative spirit in children/youth.

Note: All numbers for Bible quotes are taken from the *New American Bible*.

Accompanying children on the journey of prayer

An elderly gentleman passed his granddaughter's room one night and overheard her repeating the alphabet in an oddly reverent way. "What on earth are you up to?" he asked.

"I'm saying my prayers," explained the little girl. "But I can't think of exactly the right words tonight, so I'm just saying all the letters. God will put them together for me, because he knows what I'm thinking."

The trust of children!

And we have the privilege of accompanying them on the journey of prayer in their faith life. There is much for us to reflect on about that mystery. Let's look at just a few things:

Some prerequisites for us:

- Be a pray-er yourself. Prayer, of course, has to be part of our lives. We can't accompany others in an experience that isn't a part of us. We also need to know what we believe and value if we are going to be witnesses and have an influence on others. Many times young people will say, "I don't believe in going to church; I can pray at home just as well." I think what they're really saying is, "Tell me why you go to church."

- Constantly remind ourselves we don't "teach" children to pray. Prayer is like the common cold. It's caught, not really taught. In reality, prayer is a gift from God. As catechists, we prepare the soil, we set the environment, but prayer happens because of the relationship between the child/young person and God.

Characteristics of children/youth

In many ways, it's easy to accompany children/youth on the journey of prayer. They are natural pray-ers. They have a unique relationship with God.

- They love to pray. Once, when three of my nieces were spending the night with me, they said, "Can we do the fun prayer we did the last time?" (We had chosen things to give thanks for based on the letters of the girls' first names.) But then they changed their minds and asked me to come up with a new prayer because they now did the first one a lot at home.

- Children/youth are capable of deep prayer. During a faith formation session, an eleven-year-old boy asked, "How do I know if it's God talking to me or my own brain talking to itself?" After thinking about it for two weeks, he answered his own question, "When I get quiet after playing ball or watching TV, then it's me talking to myself. When I get empty, you know, like an empty piece of paper, then it is God."

- They know that God is real, a friend, always there. During a health test in school, a young friend of mine had this question: "Beth's mother is in the hospital and Beth feels scared. What can she do?" My friend's answer was: "She can pray for her or she can do something to get her mind off of it." It was marked wrong because the right answer was "talk to someone." Anne went to her teacher and said, "I think you should give me at least half credit. God is someone, and I talk to God all the time."

Some attitudes to develop about prayer (because that is our goal—to lead them to be prayerful people all of their lives):

- Prayer is about relationship/friendship with God. Sometimes children/youth (adults!) think of prayer either in the same category as politeness (you have to say grace before you can eat) or as a last resort in trying to get something you want. Rather, prayer is natural to life. It's who we are. We pray because we want to; we pray because we're connected to God. We can't *not* pray.

- There are all kinds of ways to pray. Prayer can be adoration, thanksgiving, sorrow, or petition. Within those four categories, there are myriad forms that prayer can take. As catechists, we have such a privilege (and responsibility) to share many different kinds of prayer with children.

- God is always with us; we just need to be aware. Sometimes our prayers ask God to "come and be with us." When we pray in that manner, I always wonder what we are teaching one another, especially our youngsters. Don't we believe that God is always with us? Perhaps our prayers need to be, "Loving God, we know you are with us. Please slow us down so we can be more aware of all the ways your love is around us today."

- Do everything you can to make prayer more personal.

   a) Simplify the language of prayer. Even inviting children/youth to pray by asking, "What are you thankful for?" might bring blank stares. You might begin by asking, "What made you happy today?" After their answers, turn those responses into a prayer of thanks.

   b) Assure children/youth that they can always tell God exactly how they feel. No feeling is beyond the realm of prayer.

- Help them to see that God and everyday happenings go together. God is not "out there." God is part of all life. Involve God in everything that happens. (We usually do a good job with sad things; why do we have a harder job with the ordinary and the happy things?)

- Lead them to understand that prayer changes us. One day, a young girl stood at a street corner begging for food, money or whatever she could get. She was wearing very tattered clothes; she was dirty and quite disheveled. A well-to-do young man passed by without giving the girl a second look. But when he returned to his expensive home, his happy family, and his bountiful table, his thoughts turned to the young girl, and he prayed to God, "How can you let this happen? Why don't you do something to help this girl?" Then he heard God respond by saying, "I did. I created you."

If we're faithful to prayer, God gives us the strength to be what we're praying for and to make a difference in the world.

Is your **catechetical time** too busy?

We inhabit a very busy and noisy world. No surprise there! Oftentimes, catechetical sessions add to the din and we may not even be aware of it. If it is the right kind of noise and activity, that can be very good. Experiential learning with lots of involvement is crucial for children/youth.

But we also have to ask ourselves: Do we pay enough attention to developing their contemplative spirit? Is there too much noise in our sessions?

What is contemplation?

Thomas Merton once said that contemplation is the highest expression of our intellectual and spiritual life. "It is spontaneous awe at the sacredness of life, of being. It is gratitude for life, for awareness, and for being. It is a vivid realization of the fact that life and being in us proceed from an invisible, transcendent and infinitely abundant source. Contemplation is, above all, awareness of the reality of that Source" (*New Seeds of Contemplation* [New York: Dell Publishing Co., 1953]).

At first glance, this description might sound very ethereal and theological. Yet it alludes to some simple but profound qualities of the human spirit: gratitude, the ability to wonder, openness to experience, the ability to be surprised.

How are these qualities nurtured? Can they be developed? I believe they can, and one of the prime ways they are nurtured is in silence. We need to allow silence into our noisy and busy world. When we enter silence, we come face to face with God: "Be still and know that I am God" (Ps 46:11). Meister Eckhart said, "Nothing in all creation is so like God as stillness."

We can do many things to help children/youth find the moments of silence that will nurture a joyous contemplative spirit:

1. Begin catechetical sessions with centering or quieting exercises which help them bridge the gap between their noisy world and this graced time. Books with numerous ideas can be found, because we are not the only ones looking for this quiet stillness; the educational field in general has seen the wisdom in using these techniques.

2. Scripture is a part of each catechetical session. Before proclaiming the Word or having a child proclaim it, have a moment of silence as everyone prepares themselves.

3. Develop prayer services (and moments in the catechetical session) where there are quiet spaces. Often, music can help to create the mood of quiet contemplation rather than just an empty space.

4. Usually it is not enough to tell children to "be quiet; pray and reflect now in silence." Their silence needs to be directed. Suggest what might happen in their quiet time:

   a) In quiet, feel God's love around you.

   b) Listen for what Jesus might want to say to you today about all the good things you have been doing.

c) In quiet, picture all the people who need your prayer today.

d) As you listen to the quiet, what are you thankful for?

e) This quiet time is so peaceful. Hand your worries over into God's hands.

5. One of my favorite introductions to quiet prayer is a visualization prayer that involves a favorite quiet place and the presence of Jesus. "Close your eyes and picture in your mind a favorite place. It might be a quiet place in your home; it may be outside in a park, near water, looking at the mountains. It could also be an imaginary place that you make up in your mind. Picture it and feel how good it is to be there. As you see yourself in your mind enjoying this place, you notice that someone is coming toward you. As he gets closer, you realize that it is Jesus. He walks over and sits beside you. He places an arm around your shoulder. Enjoy just being there with Jesus. Tell Jesus how you are feeling today, what you're happy about, what you're concerned about. Jesus is eager to hear whatever you want to tell him."

6. Use the questions below to help older children reflect on the place of silence and quiet in their lives. Who else in their world calls them to reflect on quiet and stillness and God's presence, if you don't? My experience has been that once young people have had a taste for silence and meditation, they crave it.

Am I afraid to be alone?

Am I uncomfortable doing nothing?

Have I ever spent time in solitude and silence—in a park, at the beach, some other secluded area? How did I feel?

When during my day do I experience silence?

Do I have the iPod or TV on when I do my homework, when I'm on the phone, when I'm listening to my friend?

When I have some free time, is the TV always on or do I sometimes read, pray, daydream?

After receiving communion, do I sing and pray—or watch people go by?

How much time do I allow each day for prayer? Do I do all the talking?

The "fruits" of contemplation

In nurturing the contemplative spirit in our young people, it is also crucial to help them understand (and experience) the "fruits" of contemplation. Developing a contemplative spirit spills over into all parts of our life.

There are many fruits or effects in our lives, but let's look at two that are particularly needed in the world today.

The present moment

Living life with a contemplative attitude helps us to live in the present moment.

Dr. Bernie Siegel (*Love, Medicine and Miracles*) talks about three of the characteristics of heaven: wonderful temperature, great view, and everyone lives in the present moment. He says the third one is the only one we can also have on earth.

Too many people spend ninety-four percent of their time regretting the past or planning for the future. Yet at this moment, God is not in the past or the future. God is in the present moment. If we're living in the past or future, we're missing God.

Along with developing this saner attitude toward life, we need to help our young people recognize the God that is present in our enjoyment of living. Thomas Keating once wrote that "when a person reaches a mature level of contemplative prayer, reality is seen in a new perspective. One discovers that God is present in every experience." We can help young people experience prayer that puts them in touch with living and slows them down to appreciate the presence of God at each moment.

Connecting to others

Another fruit or effect of contemplation is that it connects us with others and inspires us to involvement and action.

Too often we have equated contemplation with a withdrawal from people and activity. Nothing is further from the truth.

There is nothing inactive or passive about the contemplative way of life. Rather, it is the still point that grounds meaning and purpose in authentic human actions. Contemplation keeps us moving into the lives of people.

We do much today (and rightly so!) to motivate young people toward Christian service and connecting all of faith to their everyday world and relationships.

This needs to continue, and it will be easier if we lead our children to do it the way Jesus did: rooted in prayer and times of silence. This allows God to develop in us a sense of wonder, gratitude, and openness to the gift of each moment of life.

A a

A friend of mine was serving as eucharistic minister during Sunday liturgy. When she returned to her pew, her four-year-old granddaughter said to her, "Grandma, what were you giving all those people?" She simply explained that she was giving them Jesus.

The granddaughter, Jane, immediately responded: "Wow, that must be like swallowing sunshine!"

▶ Is there a particular form of prayer that touches you, that puts you in touch with God that concretely?

▶ How would you describe your connection with God, with Jesus, with the Spirit — because of your prayer?

Acrostic thank you prayer

The prayer of thanks can be incorporated into any session's theme by using the technique of the acrostic. Using the keyword of the theme, have each child/youth write that word down the left-hand side of a paper. For each letter, ask them to think of a person, thing, or event for which they are grateful.

During a theme on God's world, an acrostic might be:

C colors
R rivers
E eyes and ears
A animals
T time
I important people
O outer space
N north, south, east, and west

You could also use the word "thanksgiving" or each child's name. Instead of words, pictures or paintings can also illustrate the acrostic.

Acts of faith, hope, and love

Pray the Church's traditional acts of faith, hope, and love. Invite the children/youth to write their own Acts of Faith, Acts of Hope, and Acts of Love.

Add-on-prayer

This prayer is begun by inviting your learners to "add on their thoughts." The theme of the prayer can come from something that is happening in the life of the children/youth, from a current news story, or from a topic you are studying. For instance,

Leader: "Gracious God, we know you love us very much and are always with us. We want to tell you about our concerns, because we know you care for us."

Katie: "Sometimes I worry that my grandparents will die."

Each child adds his or her own current concern.

Praying with affirmations

These mini-prayers talk about the here and now with a positive approach. Some examples of affirmation prayers include: "God loves me and is always helping me." "Jesus is with me in all I do, helping me find a way to get through the hard times."

A prayer such as "I said something mean to my mom. I'm sorry; please help me make it up to her, Jesus," is a good prayer, but it is not an affirmation, because it talks about something already done (the past), and something you hope Jesus will do (in the future). "I am thinking of something nice to do for my mom. Thank you, Jesus," would be an affirmation.

Alphabet prayer

There are countless things for which we can give thanks to God. Often, of course, our thoughts go first to food, family, friends. All wonderful things, yet we want to expand our awareness, the consciousness of our young learners, to the magnitude of the gifts of our generous God. One way to do that is to brainstorm the gifts of God using the alphabet. Challenge them to pray in thanksgiving for three gifts for each letter of the alphabet: apples, aardvarks, art; brownies, buttons, and bullfrogs; dancing, doctors, dirt; llamas, latkes, and lilies.

Another variation of the Alphabet Prayer is to be alliterative, naming a gift from God, with an adjective describing it, with the same letter of the alphabet: boisterous bears; compassionate community; faithful friends; majestic mountains; rushing rivers; stunning sunsets.

For one example of an alphabet prayer, see www.cptryon. org/prayer/child/alpha.html.

The Angelus

You're probably not going to hear a church bell ring at 6:00 AM, noon, and 6:00 PM, but you can share this prayer practice with your children/youth and have them brainstorm ways it might be lived and prayed in today's world.

In 1623, the Franciscans introduced the practice of saying three Hail Marys in honor of the Incarnation. And though the custom of reciting three verses of the Angelus and three Hail Marys first appeared in the mid-sixteenth century, the version as it's now said didn't surface before the second decade of the seventeenth century. At about that time, the substitution of a different Marian prayer (the Regina Coeli) for the Angelus at Easter time was recommended and finally became the standard practice.

It also became customary that the devotion was repeated three times daily—morning, noon, and evening—at the sound of a bell.

Praying with animals

We pray, "All creation rightly gives God praise." In an imaginative way, engage the creativity of your learners, asking them how they visualize that the animals might pray to their Creator.

There are two books that are delightful, reverent, and humorous examples of this type of prayer. *How the Wild Things Pray* by William Cleary (Forest of Peace Publishing) looks at forty animals of the wild, with a poem about each animal, presumably by the animal telling us how it prays. Each animal then has an interesting footnote about its character, followed by a short meditation.

The second book is older, but there are still copies available—if not in bookstores, certainly in libraries, because it has become a classic. There have been many versions of it through the years. It is *Prayers from the Ark* by Carmen Bernos de Gasztold, translated by Rumer Godden (Viking Adult). These prayers from a selection of animals are poetic reflections on their natures, their functions, and their fates. Each creature is vividly self-characterized, wittily and concisely; at the same time, each unmistakably mirrors us! The patient, plodding ox; the awkwardly bulky elephant; the haughty cat—all pray in a way that reveals their essential weaknesses and strengths.

After exploring and enjoying these enchanting books, invite the children/youth to pretend they are various animals. What would their prayers be?

B b

Biblical prayer is impertinent, persistent, shameless, indecorous. It is more like haggling in an outdoor bazaar than the polite monologues of the church. • WALTER WINK

► Which biblical prayers have you made your own?

► When do you use biblical prayers in your catechetical sessions?

Most people do not pray; they only beg.
• GEORGE BERNARD SHAW

► What is my prayer like?

► How many forms of prayer are there?

Bible prayers

Look for simple Bible verses, especially in the psalms, that can be used as prayers of thanksgiving or sorrow. The children/youth know many of them because of the psalm refrains from the Sunday readings. They could also be encouraged to put them to simple tunes that they know: tunes from nursery rhymes, songs-known-by-everyone (e.g., campfire songs), etc.

Other verses from the Old Testament also come alive for today's world, verses such as: "O Lord, you are our Father; we are the clay and you the Potter: we are all the work of your hands" (Is 64:7).

Other verses, from various gospel persons, can also become the prayers of your children/youth: "O God, be merciful to me…" (Lk 18:13); "Lord, I want to see" (Mk 10:51); Jesus, my Lord, my God, my All (Jn 20:28); or various prayers from the Letters: "We pray we may live a life worthy of the Lord and may please him in every way: bearing fruit in every good work, growing in the knowledge of God, being strengthened with all power according to his glorious might so that we may have great endurance and patience, and joyfully giving thanks to the Father, who has qualified us to share in the inheritance of the saints in the kingdom of light" (Col 1:9–12).

The magnificent Scripture Canticles are prayers the children/youth can pray and treasure. They are:

- the Magnificat (Mary's song of praise, spoken during her visit to her cousin Elizabeth when Elizabeth praises Mary for her faith)

- the Benedictus (the Canticle of Zachary, uttered by Zachary on the birth of his son, John the Baptist)

- the Nunc Dimittis (the Canticle of Simeon, who took Jesus into his arms when Mary and Joseph brought Jesus to the temple forty days after his birth; Simeon had been promised he would not die until he had seen the Messiah)

Blessings

"To be blessed" means "to be favored by God." To express a blessing is like bestowing a wish on someone that he/she will experience the favor of God. "May you have a blessed Christmas," therefore can be translated as: "May you experience the favor of God during this Christmas period."

It is God who blesses. To pray a prayer of blessing, we are not "doing" the blessing. We are praying and—as always—believing in God's action with us and for/with those for whom we are praying. One of the first incidences of blessing in Scripture is in Genesis 12:1–2 where Abraham is ordered by God to leave his country and is told: "I will bless you, I will make your name great."

As we go throughout our day—our catechetical "day"—we never run out of times and places for blessings. Begin your time together with a blessing: "May the Lord be with you." "And also with you." At times, invite one of the children/youth to pray a prayer of blessing as your session begins.

Prayers of blessings are beautiful, personal, and affirming experiences of God's love and your concern for your learners, especially when you place your hands on them as you pray. An end-of-class blessing might also incorporate the use of holy water, recalling God's protection and care for all people. "Our time together has ended. Go in peace." "Thanks be to God."

Teach the children/youth ways to bless their families, to write blessings for their families, for parish shut-ins and the grieving, for those celebrating sacraments, anniversaries and special occasions. The blessing for their families can be lettered, decorated, and framed so that it can be hung prominently in their homes and prayed frequently.

During a lesson on reaching out, serving, and making a difference in the world (which each lesson should end with), invite the children/youth to bless each other's hands with holy water or oil.

As you use blessing prayers, vary them so they don't become rote, without any meaning.

At times, write your own; at other times, use blessings from the words of the Mass, our sacraments, and the rites of the RCIA. Another rich source is *Catholic Household Blessings and Prayers* (USCCB Publications, www.usccbpublishing.org), which, among many other occasions, contains blessings for family members, during sickness, during childhood, and for our sacramentals (e.g., Advent wreath, Christmas crib, candles, etc.).

Your group could search out various blessing prayers for family situations to be compiled into a booklet. The booklets could be copied—one for each family. These could be presented, with a bottle of holy water, to each family during a family prayer service. Families are looking for ways to pray together. This—because of the ritual, and the power of touch—provides an opportunity for families that is simple but will affect and bond them, as well as providing the "God moments" for which they search.

Prayer boxes

Various kinds of boxes can be used for this prayer activity. Sometimes the types of boxes in which carry-outs or leftovers from Chinese restaurants are placed are perfect. (Many times the restaurants will donate them to you, or you can purchase them from them economically.) Tissue boxes are also good. Of course, purchasing small square or uniquely shaped boxes from a packaging or stationery store works well, too.

This work of prayer is to create a prayer box that each child/youth will take home to be placed on the family dinner table. Inside will be various prayers that can be pulled out at dinner time to be prayed together by the family.

To complete this project, you may want to have it take place over time, giving the children/youth plenty of time to find/

decide on the prayers they would like to put into their boxes, rather than doing it all at once.

Some ideas for the prayers that might be included and suggested to the young learners: Give the children/youth copies of various prayers, such as our Church's traditional prayers (Our Father, Hail Mary, the Angelus, Glory Be, etc.), as well as many ideas for blessings before meals, especially from various cultures and traditions. Include also in this copy other prayers for families, blessings for families, prayers for various family times and family situations. They would then cut from the copy all of the prayers they would like to include in their prayer box and place them inside.

Have available, in your group meeting space, various books of prayers and blessings so that—throughout the weeks devoted to this prayer activity—the children and youth might browse through these books and find other prayers they think their family would like. Provide them with blank paper to copy these prayers and add them to their prayer box.

Encourage them to surf the Internet for meal prayers, family prayers, prayers of the Catholic family. When they find others that they would like for their family, print them and add them to their family prayer box.

Suggest that they include blank sheets of paper in the prayer box. On a day when their family pulls out one of these slips of paper, they make up their own prayer—right then and there. They might choose to write the new prayer on that paper and add it to the prayer box, for a future time.

The outside of the prayer box can be decorated with two or three short prayers or with pictures or symbols of prayer.

The breathing prayer

Invite children/youth to begin the habit of breathing in God's love and breathing out anything that might be worrying them.

Breathe in the courage of God…
breathe out any fears.

Breathe in the forgiveness and strength of God…
breathe out any grudges and anger.

Breathe in God's joy and peace…
breathe out any sadness you may feel inside yourself.

Breathe in the compassion of God…
breathe out any selfishness.

Each time they take a breath, encourage the children/youth to feel the unconditional love of God surrounding them, filling them, empowering them. Thus, another version might be:

Breathe in the love of Christ…
breathe out tension and worry.

Breathe in the love of Christ…
breathe out fear and concerns.

Breathe in the love of Christ…
breathe out negativity and pessimism.

Breathe in the love of Christ…
breathe out anger or resentment.

C c

A five-year-old said grace at family dinner one night. "Dear God, thank you for these pancakes." When he concluded, his parents asked him why he thanked God for pancakes when they were having chicken. He smiled and said, "I thought I'd see if God was paying attention tonight."

▶ Do we ever wonder if God is paying attention?

▶ Might we be the one who is not paying attention?

Praying with a camera

Several years ago, there was a wonderful book that told how a village grade school in Hawaii was saved from closure and revitalized when the students, parents, and teachers took a field trip to find God (*God's Photo Album* by Shelly Mecum, HarperSanFrancisco, 2001).

Armed with cameras, the students, teachers, and parents set out around the island of Oahu — prayerfully and reflectively — to look at people, circumstances, things in a new way: Where did they see God? Then they wrote their reflections.

Invite your young pray-ers to do the same thing. The question could be posed in different ways, at different times:

- Where do you see God?

- Where do you see compassion alive?

- Where are places for prayer?

- Where is peace?

Prayer captains

Invite each child/youth to take a turn at being the "prayer captain" for your group, leading the prayer for your session for a particular day. The prayer captain can choose the prayer for the day from scriptural prayer or from a book of children/youth prayers, or can compose the prayer personally.

This method is an effective way of involving families with their children in sharing faith, because the composing—and/or the searching for the prayer—can be a family project.

A prayer time capsule

A prayer time capsule can be a group activity that would encourage reflection upon our prayer, resulting in increasing gratitude and trust in God. Each person is invited to write a prayer to God. The prayer mentions any challenges or questions that the person might be facing at the present time. The prayer asks God's help with these problems.

All these prayers can be placed in a large envelope or box that's labeled "Prayer Time Capsule." A special date is chosen (at least several months away) for the opening of the package. Together, the group thanks God for knowing what will work out for the best in each one of their lives.

Centering prayer

Centering prayer was developed more than seventeen centuries ago to help people with the important part of prayer: listening. It has been reintroduced to Western society as a prayer form in itself. It is a prayer in which we rest in God's presence and attempt to be as quiet and still as we can. During centering prayer, we are invited to simply be and enjoy God's loving us.

The guidelines are meant to be simple. In today's busy world, children/youth embrace centering prayer easily and find it inviting and appealing to be centered with God.

The guidelines are:

1. Find a quiet place to sit.

2. Choose a word (or phrase) that for you is a sign that you want God to be present and active within you. Think of it as your "invitation word." Some possibilities might be Jesus, Lord, Father, Spirit, be still, peace, Resurrection, Love, etc.

3. Sit comfortably and repeat your invitation word peacefully and gently. Let your mind and soul settle into a listening silence.

4. If you become aware of wandering or distracting thoughts during your prayer time, gently go back to your invitation word.

5. Simply be in quiet and silence and enjoy God's loving you.

6. Conclude your prayer time with a few moments of silence. Alternatively, you may end by slowly reciting the Our Father, the Hail Mary, or the Glory Be.

Most writers recommend practicing centering prayer for two twenty-minute periods a day—once early in the day and again around the time of the evening meal—to gain the maximum benefit. Shorter prayer times, or practicing it once a day, can still be beneficial.

When centering prayer is done in a group (as in your catechetical setting), the leader might say or lead a prayer to the Holy Spirit asking for the Spirit's guidance and help during the prayer time. Gentle, flowing background music might be played during the prayer time, if it is not distracting to the participants. The leader would initiate the recitation of the prayer chosen to conclude the session.

Chants

In our tradition, chanting has had a rich heritage in prayer practices. Chanting is the rhythmic speaking or singing of words or sounds, often primarily on one or two pitches called reciting tones. Children/youth love music and enjoy responding in song.

We can utilize many of the hymns written in chant form or we can invite our learners to write their own: Chant a psalm or a line from other Scripture, or write a personal prayer and put it into chant (e.g., "Thank you, Lord, for your constant presence with us.").

Often today, some chants are short hymns—short lines from Scripture—which are chanted over and over again, serving as a meditative hymn to help our bodies and minds peacefully slow down and remind us we are in God's presence.

Praying through a cinquain

Using the form of a cinquain poem to write a prayer can be a help to many children/young people in focusing their thoughts and reflections. Individuals might do their own, or small groups might work together on one.

The guidelines for writing a cinquain are:

A cinquain poem has five lines, the word coming from the French *cinq*, which means "five." The rules for writing them are based on syllables. Cinquain poems have the following pattern:

Line 1: two syllables
Line 2: four syllables
Line 3: six syllables
Line 4: eight syllables
Line 5: two syllables

An alternate version of the cinquain poem, often called a "word cinquain," is based on words instead of syllables. "Word cinquains" have the following pattern:

Line 1: one word
Line 2: two words
Line 3: three words
Line 4: four words
Line 5: one word

There are no specific rules for writing a cinquain except that it must have five lines and the correct syllable count (or, if it's a word cinquain, the correct word count).

However, there are many suggestions for writing a good cinquain. The suggestion of mixing the emphasis of the syllables (or words) will create a stronger effect than writing a string of words with similar lengths and emphasis. Other poetic devices such as assonance and alliteration can be used to help make cinquain poems memorable. Organizing the ideas in a cinquain to follow the order below is another suggestion:

- title
- description of the title
- some action about the title

- feeling about the title
- synonym (similar word) for the title

The topics related to faith, belief, creed, and spirituality that can be prayed about in a cinquain poem are endless. Your children/youth's depth of prayer could find a home here.

Collect graces

Grace before meals is a favorite way to pray in most families (or one that we, as catechists, can encourage). Help your learners to research and compile into a booklet various graces from different cultures, traditions, peoples, and places. Make copies of the booklet so each child/youth has one to take home.

Colorful prayers

There's an enchanting children's classic, a book of poetry called *Hailstones and Halibut Bones*. Read one of the poems—which tells about one of the colors in God's world. Invite your children/youth to write a prayer thanking God for that particular color in the world. They might want to mention:

- where and when they see that color

- why they like that color

- how they—and others—use that color

Come, Holy Spirit

This prayer—one of the most well-known that's prayed to the Holy Spirit—is used by the Church at Vespers, Pentecost, the Dedication of a Church, the celebration of Confirmation, and Holy Orders.

During catechetical sessions, it can easily be used within a longer prayer service or as a prayer by itself, helping children/youth focus on the constant role of the Holy Spirit in their lives.

Come Holy Spirit, fill the hearts of your faithful and kindle in them the fire of your love.

V. Send forth your Spirit, and they shall be created.

R. And You shall renew the face of the earth.

Let us pray…

O God, who by the light of the Holy Spirit, did instruct the hearts of the faithful, grant that by the same Holy Spirit we may be truly wise and ever enjoy His consolations. Through Christ our Lord. Amen.

Prayer of cooperation

Often in Scripture, the apostles suggested something to Jesus, such as in this episode: "Send the crowd away so they can go to the surrounding villages and countryside and find food and lodging." Jesus' response to his friends was, "You give them something to eat" (Lk 9:12–13).

This happens in our lives of prayer today, too. Jesus invites us to cooperate with him, to be partners with him, often to be an answer to our own prayers.

Help your learners not simply to tell God that someone is in need and ask God to alleviate that need, but also to spend time in prayer listening, just in case God is suggesting that we send a get-well card, or take the first step in forgiving or making peace.

You might want to read the prologue "Partners" in *Does God Have a Big Toe? Stories about Stories in the Bible* by Marc Gellman (HarperTrophy).

Prayer through creativity

As many of the prayers throughout this book illustrate, prayer expresses itself in many ways, not only words. God gave us many gifts, countless gifts of imagination and originality. Invite your children/youth to pray with their talents:

- Make a design of what you imagine peace looks like.

- Create a dance that shows your joy at being created by such a loving God.

- Mold a piece of clay to show your relationship with God.

- Sketch a billboard to show the world's litany of thanks.

D d

Dear God, I think about you sometimes even when I'm not praying. • ELLIOTT, WWW.CATHOLICLINKS.ORG/ CTOSILETTERSTOGOD.HTM, ACCESSED AUGUST 1, 2010

▶ What helps you think about God throughout the day, even while you're not praying?

▶ Have you ever asked your children/youth this question?

Departure rituals

Leave-taking and the rituals that accompany it are very important, or should be! As we come to the end of each of our sessions, we can use these ending moments to send the children/youth on their way with prayerful rituals.

You might choose to close the session with a group prayer and ritual; then, as your learners leave, stand at the door and personally send forth each person. Bless each one, tracing the Sign of the Cross on his/her forehead. If you have access to holy water, use that; or make the Sign of the Cross on the palms of their hands.

Pray a prayer of blessing for each, such as, "May you walk with Jesus during your coming week."

Share the Sign of Peace with each child/youth as he or she leaves.

Doodle-your-feelings prayer

Prayer is much more than words. Provide your learners with paint, felt-tip markers, colored chalk, or crayons. Lead the children/youth in prayer: "God who loves us, You have given me so many people to love. This is how I feel when I think of my family….This is how I feel when I think of my friends…."

The children/youth are invited to pray their feelings with color, with design, with symbols. The idea is not to "draw a picture," but simply to pray their feelings. What they do could simply be a blob of color, or it could be symbolic; it should be whatever helps them to pray, sharing their feelings with God.

The lead-in sentences that you use can be about all areas of the learners' lives: questions and concerns that might be on their minds and in their hearts; thoughts flowing from topics you are currently studying; etc.

Drawing prayer

Now this idea *is* to draw a picture. There's probably no home in the country that doesn't have pictures, drawings, paintings that children have done for their parents. Invite children to draw a picture for God, their loving parent, telling God about something they're excited about, something they're concerned about, their dreams for the world, etc.

E e

A small boy had a rough day, spending most of it involved in mischief. When his frustrated father put him to bed that evening and told him to say his prayers, the little boy said, "Dad, I'd like you to leave. I want to talk with God alone tonight."

"Why? What have you done that you don't want me to know about?" the now-more-than-ever-annoyed father asked.

"If I tell you," the small boy said, "you'll get angry and probably shout and yell. But I know God will listen, forgive me and forget about it."

▶ How often does your prayer include prayer of sorrow, prayer of reconciliation?

▶ Prayer of reconciliation also includes reconciliation with those we've hurt. Is that difficult for you?

With me, prayer is a lifting up of the heart, a look towards heaven, a cry of gratitude and love uttered equally in sorrow and joy; in a word, something noble, supernatural, which enlarges my soul and unites it to God.

• SAINT THÉRÈSE OF LISIEUX

> ► Does prayer make your life larger, deeper?

> ► Does your prayer of thanks come at times of sorrow, at times of joy — or both?

Echo prayer

The echo prayer is a simple form of prayer, especially appealing to younger children. The children repeat a prayer, phrase by phrase, after the catechist. For young children, this beginning type of prayer can acquaint them with the language and form of prayer, giving them ideas for future prayers of their own.

Enthronement of the Bible

Begin each of your sessions with an Enthronement of Scripture. Involve all children/youth in the procession as you move to your prayer space, carrying the Bible. As you reach the table, the participants can form two lines on either side. The Bible bearer, who is last in the procession, reverently places the book in its place while everyone sings a refrain.

This song can be one of the psalm refrains from Sunday liturgy, or one that the children/youth have written themselves.

At times, children may show reverence for the Scriptures before leaving the prayer space to gather for the session: tracing the Sign of the Cross on the open Scriptures, bowing before the Bible, etc.

Everyday psalm prayers

During a study on the psalms, the children/youth will learn, of course, that these prayers were the "everyday prayers" of the

Jewish people. They prayed about anything and everything that was on their minds, all that was occurring in their everyday lives—there was nothing they could not bring to their God.

Invite your children/youth to write their own everyday psalms. What are their joys, dreams, worries, concerns, fears, needs, hopes? They can write these without placing their names on them.

You can place them in a large box or bag and periodically during a prayer time, invite two or three children/youth to randomly take out two or three prayers to become part of your prayer. For youth who are hesitant to share their prayers, no one would know which prayer belongs to whom.

Another alternative is to place these prayers on a PowerPoint; again, periodically two or three of the prayers can be used within a prayer time, with all of the children/youth praying them together—or the pray-ers can be divided into smaller groups praying different portions of the prayer.

Prayer with everyday objects

Use any and all kinds of everyday objects. The ideal would be to give each child/youth an object to hold. Some possible objects: a penny, an apple, a piece of tree bark, something soft, a chunk of bread, bandages, something with a wonderful smell, a seashell, a stone, cherries, something made of linen, a feather, a jar of lotion, etc.

Invite your learners, knowing that God is with them, to close their eyes and take time to wonder at and appreciate all that surrounds them. Invite them to touch the item in their hand, keeping their eyes closed. Feel the object in every way possible. Is it cool or warm? Soft or rough? Natural or made by people?

Think of how the object is useful. Could it help someone who is sick or needy? Could it help get something done? Has it ever protected something or someone? Who needs it? Why do you think God created it, or why do you think humans made it?

Using the object, invite your learners to make up a prayer of thanksgiving.

Prayer from everyday symbols

Invite your learners to look around your meeting space and choose three objects that they see. Think about each object— what it is, what it does, what it symbolizes, how they use it, what it reminds them of. Now, using those three objects, invite them to compose a prayer. (For instance, using a paper cup, a key and a book, a prayer might be: "Lord God, fill my heart with your love; open my life to others so that I might share your Word with them. Amen.")

Examen of Consciousness

The Examen (not the same as the Examination of Conscience) is a prayer that helps us meet Jesus in our daily lives, as he encourages us to do God's will. People are encouraged to pray this reflective prayer twice a day. We can introduce it to our children/youth, using it frequently in our sessions and supporting them in their use of it in their personal and family prayer time.

The five steps of the Examen are:

1. Presence: We're always in the presence of God. At this time of prayer, I'm slowing down to become aware of how close God is to me.

2. Thanksgiving: Today, for what things am I most grateful? Become aware of things I might usually miss.

3. Help: Ask help from the Holy Spirit.

4. Review: When did I love? When did I fail? Why?

5. Reconcile and Resolve: Talk with Jesus about what has happened, my feelings, and my plans for tomorrow.

Examination of Conscience

An examination of conscience is a way to hold ourselves accountable before God and each other for the failings/sins we do and the good we do not do.

We have, as Catholic Christians, several guidelines for our lives, ways to live as Jesus did. The Ten Commandments give us a crucial blueprint; Jesus also challenged us with the guidelines of the Beatitudes (Matthew 5:1–12). Certainly, other sayings and teachings of Jesus also call us to a life of discipleship, such as the Lord's Prayer (Luke 11:2–4) and the Last Judgment (Matthew 25:31–46).

An examination of conscience can be incorporated into a prayer service or stand alone as your prayer time. You, as catechist, could prepare the examination of conscience, or your young learners could write the examination, especially based upon a specific theme you have been studying.

This could be an examination of conscience flowing from the Lord's Prayer:

Our Father, who art in heaven, hallowed be Thy name
- How is God a part of my life?
- When do I pray?
- What is my favorite way of praying?
- How do I participate in Sunday liturgy at my parish?
- How do I live the liturgy when I leave the church building?

Thy kingdom come, Thy will be done on earth as it is in heaven.
- What do I think Jesus is calling me to do?
- How do I make my home a peaceful place?
- When was I kind last week?
- Would people say I'm a respectful person?
- What are the gifts I have that I share with others?
- How have I made the world around me a better place?

Give us this day our daily bread
- How often during the day do I say "Thank you"?
- Whom do I thank?
- Do I sometimes want more than I need?
- How do I show appreciation for the wonderful things I have in my life?
- How do I help people who are needy?
- Am I respectful of things that belong to other people?

Forgive us our trespasses as we forgive those who trespass against us.
- Do I apologize to others when I have hurt them, when I have been wrong?
- Do I forgive when someone does something to me? Do I forget?
- Do I gossip? Do I say cruel things about people who have hurt me?

Lead us not into temptation, but deliver us from evil
- In games and sports, do I play fairly?
- Am I honest in all I say and do?
- In all my actions, am I setting a good example?
- Am I strong and do I follow my values, or do I let others tempt me to do things I shouldn't do?

Praying through the eyes of others

Sometimes older youth are self-conscious about composing a prayer or praying spontaneously and expressing their own feelings. Collect articles for your learners from the Internet or newspapers, articles that tell about several happenings, various real-life situations, such as an accident, a success story, the beginning of an important project, a racial incident, etc. Invite the children/youth to compose the kind of prayer the person(s) in the articles might pray in that situation.

This would be less threatening, yet they are learning two important things: how to compose a prayer; and the fact that prayer is appropriate in all life situations.

F f

A pastor asked a little boy if he said his prayers every night.

"Yes, sir," the boy replied.

"And do you always say them in the morning, too?" the pastor asked.

"No, Father," the boy replied, "I ain't scared in the daytime."

▶ When have you prayed because you were afraid?

▶ In your life, what is the reason for prayer?

Faith sharing

Sharing faith can be an integral part of prayer time. It is prayerful, insightful, ever-deepening, and respectful of others. Many times it will flow from the Scripture reading; at times you might pose a question flowing from what is happening in your learners' everyday lives, in the life of your group, in what you are studying. This can be a faith question, such as:

• How would you describe Jesus to a person who has never heard of him?

• What if Jesus returned to earth tomorrow?

41

- Do you know Jesus well enough to predict what he'd say and do if he joined you during a typical day?

- What if Jesus said to you, "What do you want me to do for you?"

- Would you rather attend the Last Supper or discover Jesus' empty tomb?

- The Bible character I'd most like to be like is _____ .

- The Bible character I'd least like to be like is _____ .

- The person in the gospels most like me is _____ .

- The one thing that makes me sure there's a God is _____ .

- Other than Jesus, I think _____ is the greatest person who ever lived.

- The dream I have which I would most like to see come true is _____ .

Fantasy trip

Invite your children to enter into a fantasy trip: "Pretend you are with God before the world was made. It is dark and cold. God puts out his hand and says, 'Let there be light.' Then God makes the sun. See how beautiful and bright the sun is. Feel how warm it is on your face…."

Another type of fantasy prayer would be to read a gospel story to your learners. Then invite them to pretend that they are the people in the story. "Pretend you are the people Jesus fed with the loaves and fishes. How do you feel? What do you say to him?" Depending upon the age of your children/youth and the theme of the particular gospel story, their responses may be written, kept personal, or shared.

Five-finger prayer

This prayer help is from an anonymous author, being used frequently to help pray-ers remember various people who need our prayers.

1. Your thumb is nearest you. So begin your prayers by praying for those closest to you. They are the easiest to remember. To pray for our loved ones, as C.S. Lewis once said, is a "sweet duty."

2. The next finger is the pointing finger. Pray for those who teach, instruct, and heal. This includes teachers, doctors, and ministers. They need support and wisdom in pointing others in the right direction. Keep them in your prayers.

3. The next finger is the tallest finger. It reminds us of our leaders. Pray for the president, leaders in business and industry, and administrators. These people shape our nation and guide public opinion. They need God's guidance.

4. The fourth finger is our ring finger. Surprising to many is the fact that this is our weakest finger, as any piano teacher will testify. It should remind us to pray for those who are weak, in trouble, or in pain. They need your prayers day and night. You cannot pray too much for them.

5. And last comes our little finger, the smallest finger of all. This is where we should place ourselves in relation to God and others. As the Bible says, "The least shall be the greatest among you." Your pinkie should remind you to pray for yourself. By the time you have prayed for the other four groups, you will realize that your own needs probably are not as great as the needs of others. You will be able to pray for yourself much better since you have taken the time to pray for others first.

G g

A five-year-old boy was sitting down to eat when his mother asked him to say the prayer before dinner. He replied, "Mom, we don't have to. We prayed over this last night." His mother had prepared leftovers from the day before.

- ▶ Are there times we might think we don't need to pray right now? We prayed yesterday, or Sunday, or last week…and today is just like yesterday. What could be new?
- ▶ What do you do when it feels hard to pray?
- ▶ How will you talk with your children/youth about the times in life when it feels "not necessary" to pray?

Since when are words the only acceptable form of prayer?
• DOROTHY DAY

- ▶ What else might Dorothy be thinking of?
- ▶ In what other ways have you prayed, in addition to words?

General intercessions

Helping our children and young people compose and pray intercessory prayers, built upon the structure of the general intercessions of our liturgy, can be a benefit to their prayer life as well as our life together as a eucharistic community.

This "prayer of the faithful" was never, in the history of the liturgy, understood as the prayer *for* the faithful. These prayers are never just for ourselves. They are for the needs and concerns of the whole Church, of the whole world. That is why the preferred title for these prayers is "general intercessions."

The *General Instruction on the Roman Missal* guides the categories for our general intercessions at liturgy:

- prayers for the needs of the church

- prayers for public authorities and the salvation of the world

- prayers for those oppressed by any need

- prayers for the local community

When we're praying in this format, a few other guidelines direct these prayers:

- These are prayers of petition. It is not appropriate to compose them in a style that reflects other prayer forms, such as thanksgiving or adoration.

- Genuine necessities, real needs, should be the subject of the petitions. Current events should help shape the intercessions.

- Rather than telling God what to do, these intercessions ask God for guidance in doing God's will. Rather than expecting God to take action, we ask God to move and strengthen us to do what God desires.

- At times, in formulating the prayers, we might draw from the verbs or other action words of the Scripture readings.

Genesis prayers

This prayer is adapted from an idea for morning prayer: Genesis (beginning) prayer, or prayer of the first four minutes of the day. We can encourage our young people to make this a part of their day, the first four minutes of their day, the first four minutes before they get out of bed. Adapted for our use, it can be the first four minutes of our session together.

If it is morning prayer, before even getting out of bed, remember that God is with you. Give thanks for another day that will be filled with gifts, surprises, opportunities for life, kindness, care. How will you choose to live this day: alone — or with others, with God? What can you do this day to bring a little more joy, a little more gentleness, compassion, peace to your world?

If you use this at the beginning of your catechetical session, it can be adapted to the seasonal or current happenings of your group. Recall the many ways God has been with each person during that day. Give thanks for the day, the past week that has been filled with wonders, with amazing surprises, with opportunities of enjoying God's gifts of family, friendship, learning, people who care, etc. We have before us now this holy time — with this community of God's people, our special friends. How will each of us listen, pray, share with one another so that we can grow to be better followers of Jesus and light up our world?

Praying through geometric shapes

It is so fascinating that everything can tell us something about God, everything can lead us to prayer.

Our world is filled with lines, circles, rectangles, pentagons, ovals, triangles, octagons, trapezoids, crescents, etc. Focus on a specific shape during a prayer time. You might have one large shape that each child/youth can touch, feel, explore; or you could have many smaller ones so that each can have their own. As they explore it, guide them through a prayerful reflection with questions, such as:

- Does this shape play a role in my life?

- Does this shape tell me something about myself?

- Might this shape tell me something about my prayer? about the way I usually pray? about the way I like to pray?

- Does this shape remind me of things, tell me about things in God's world?

- Is God like this shape in any way?

- What might this shape teach me about God?

Invite the children/youth to take any of their thoughts or reflections and compose a prayer to God.

Prayer with gestures

Gestures, body movements that accompany words, have always had a place in prayer. 2 Samuel 6:14–15 tells us that David danced before the Ark of the Lord. Psalm 63:5 prays "Lifting up my hands, I will call upon your name."

The early Church fathers called Jesus the Lord of the Dance. Saint Jerome said, "The joy of the Spirit finds expression in bodily gestures."

Gestures intensify the meaning of our prayer words, any words. As non-hearing people remind us, gestures intensify what we're saying. We mean it more when we use our bodies to say it.

Many of the catechists' guides give suggestions and ideas for gestures to accompany our formal prayers, such as the Our Father, the Hail Mary, the Glory Be.

Your learners can be invited to design their own gestures for these prayers, as well as gestures for their own personally written prayers. As they reflect on the Sunday readings, invite them, in small groups, to design gestures for the refrain of the psalm response.

The prayer glove

With younger children, take a glove, decorate it simply, numbering each finger. During prayer time, whoever would like to offer a prayer puts on the glove and mentions five things—such as five things for which they are grateful, five people for whom they would like to pray, five kinds of help they need from God right now, etc.

You might choose to have a different glove for different themes: A "Count Your Blessings" glove is only for praying about the five things for which you are grateful; a "We Care for Others" glove is only for praying for the needs of others, etc.

Guided Scripture meditations

It is one thing to help our young people study Scripture, understanding what happened, the meaning of the passage, why the author included it, etc. That is very important in our catechetical ministry. The key question is: Where am I in this story? What does this mean in my life? What is Jesus saying to me right now? What does Jesus want me to do now?

Guided Scripture meditations—which we can do within the catechetical setting—are prayerful times for the children/youth then and there; they are also teaching them this method that they can do continually on their own.

Invite your young learners into a quiet space—both physically within your room and within their own bodies and minds. Invite them to the time when Jesus lived on earth: let them listen as you reverently read one of the stories from Scripture. Ask them to become part of the story. They may choose to be one of the people mentioned in the story, or they can remain themselves and enter into the story. Notice the sights, colors, sounds, smells, and tastes of the place. How do they feel about being here? About being this close to Jesus?

Invite them to pay attention to their feelings—about themselves, about the other people in the story, about Jesus. What are they hearing Jesus say? What are they seeing Jesus do? What is Jesus saying to them? What is Jesus saying about their lives?

Invite them—when the story is over—to take quiet time to talk with Jesus. Then sit in silence and listen. What is Jesus saying to them?

After they have had enough time, invite them to thank Jesus and say good-bye—knowing that Jesus is always with them—and slowly return to your time and place. You may wish to begin praying the Our Father or Glory Be, with the children/youth joining you.

At times, you may wish to give your learners a chance to debrief this experience. "What happened to you as you listened to the Scripture story? Are there parts of this prayer that you liked? Why? Do you have any questions?"

H h

A first-grade class presented a Nativity play shortly before Christmas. When Joseph came to the inn and knocked on the door, meeting the innkeeper, he inquired if there was room at the inn.

The little boy playing the innkeeper immediately replied, "You're very lucky. We just had a cancellation."

▶ Is there always room in the inn of your heart for Jesus, no matter when he shows up? (In reality, he's always there, but there may be times he shows up in the guise of phone calls that interrupt, an irritable family member, the needy, etc.)

▶ Is this prayer?

Hallel prayer

When we sing the chorus "Hallelu, hallelu, hallelu, halleluia," we are singing the Jewish words for "Praise the Lord." In the psalms are several chapters known as the "Hallel" chapters. These chapters, Psalms 146–150, are also called the Praise Chapters. The Hebrew words for "Praise the Lord" are "Hallelu Yah," which we spell "halleluia" or "alleluia."

Invite your children/youth to look at Psalms 146–150, paying attention to the first and last sentences of each chapter. Then, notice what the psalmist is praising God for in each of these chapters.

After reflecting on these Jewish psalms, invite the children/youth to write their own Hallel. Suggest that they begin and end it with "Praise the Lord." Write several lines praising God's goodness, love, unfailing kindness, compassion, or whichever characteristics of God they would want to mention.

Prayer helps

Often our learners are supported in their prayer by simple helps, which assist them to organize their ideas for prayer, such as:

- A "prayer bottle" (an empty wine bottle) can be covered with magazine pictures and words on a given theme, such as the people in our lives, the gifts of nature, times of forgiveness, working for justice, etc. During prayer time, pass the bottle from child to child and invite each of them to offer a prayer when the bottle is passed to them. They may do it aloud or silently.

- Two prayer boxes, with prayers of thanks and prayers of petition, can have a permanent place in your meeting area. Learners are encouraged to write their prayers on 3 x 5 cards and place them in the appropriate boxes. Periodically, the boxes can be opened so the prayers can be incorporated into the prayer of your group during your gathering times.

- Prayer chain links can be made by your children/youth, with each link representing one thing for which they are thankful. As these are stapled onto the chain, a prayer of thanks can be prayed. The prayer chain could also be the people, situations, and intentions in the world for which the children are praying. This idea also can be adapted and used for a liturgical season, such as Lent or Easter.

I i

Who one believes God to be is most accurately revealed not in any credo but in the way one speaks to God when no one else is listening. • NANCY MAIRS

▶ In your personal prayer time, how do you and God talk?

▶ What do you believe about God?

I believe

The Creed is foundational for us as Catholics. Pray one (or both) of our Creeds (Nicene and Apostles).

Following a study of the Creed, invite your learners to compose and/or voice their own prayers of statements of belief. One type of creed could be statements of belief about themselves, the church, and God.

Another approach would be to divide your group into four smaller groups, inviting each group to work on one of the areas or topics that are the traditional divisions of a creed: God, Jesus, the Holy Spirit, and the church. Each group could be invited to write about four or five statements to convey their belief and understanding of their topic area. When each group has finished, put them together for a complete creed, written by your group.

On another day, you can do the exercise again (without this creed in sight) and have different learners in each group. Do different representations of belief and understanding, different ways of expressing ourselves in prayer, result from this?

Imagine

Encourage the children/youth to reflect on prayer—their ways of prayer—by imagining. "Imagine that you are the first person who ever prayed. What do you think moved you to pray? Where are you? What and who do you see? What is your prayer?"

Because children/youth love to live in their imaginations, capitalize on this by inviting them to think of their favorite place—real or made up. During prayer time, have them meet Jesus in this favorite place. With guiding questions, help children/youth develop these times into intimate conversations and listening opportunities with Jesus: How are they feeling? For what are they grateful? What is on their minds and touching their hearts? Invite them to talk with—and then listen to—Jesus.

Pray with incense

Remind the children/youth that the sweet smell of incense helps us remember that prayer time is a unique part of our day. The psalms tell us that our prayers rise like incense to our God.

In the Church's Liturgy of the Hours, during the gospel canticle at Morning Prayer and Evening Prayer, incense may be used to cense the altar, the priest, and congregation.

During our celebration of liturgy, incense may be used during the entrance procession; at the beginning of Mass, to cense the altar; at the procession and proclamation of the gospel; at the offertory, to cense the offerings, altar, priest, and people. During funeral Masses, the priest at the final commendation may cense the coffin, both as a sign of honor to the body of the deceased — which became the temple of the Holy Spirit at baptism — and as a sign of the faithful's prayers for the deceased rising to God.

In our prayer space, incense may be used, at times, to help us remember the words of the psalmist: "Let my prayer come like incense before you; the lifting up of my hands, like the evening sacrifice" (141:2). It can simply sit on your prayer table, or also be used to cense the Scriptures and reverently cense the children/ youth.

In thanksgiving of our goodness

Invite your children/youth to think reverently about and name some of the good things, characteristics, and gifts of God that they see in each of the other children/youth in their group.

Once this has been done, work with them, helping them to write these ideas into a litany-style prayer in which each person is mentioned and praised for his/her gifts, characteristics, unique qualities. The completed prayer can be typed up, with a copy given to each child/youth, so that it can be prayed at home with their families.

Certainly, it can be a part of your group prayer periodically throughout the year, as you remember — and thank God for — the specialness of each person gathered within this group.

J j

A man was lost in the desert. Later, when describing his ordeal to his friends, he told how, in sheer desperation, he had knelt down and cried out to God to help him.

"And did God answer your prayer?" they asked.

"Oh, no!" the man said. "Before he could, an explorer appeared out of nowhere and showed me the way."

▶ Is my life so busy that sometimes I don't recognize all the God moments?

▶ Do I expect God only in certain places, in specific ways—and therefore miss all the breathtaking ways God is constantly with me?

▶ When I pray, do I have it all planned how I want my prayer "answered," thereby missing God's marvelous plans?

The Jesus Prayer

This is an ancient Christian contemplative prayer consisting of short phrases prayed over and over again in order for us to quiet down and become more aware of God's presence. The most common phrase is "Lord Jesus Christ, Son of God, have mercy on me, a sinner." Sometimes it is shortened to "Jesus, mercy" or simply the name "Jesus."

Another simple version is to take a deep breath. As you inhale, mentally say, "Je-"; and as you exhale, pray, "-sus." With each breath repeat the name Jesus.

People will say the reason for this prayer is to get rid of or suspend all our thoughts, but it's not really that. The purpose of it (as of all prayer) is to help us encounter our loving God, to help us slow down and be more aware of how close our God is to us.

Invite your young pray-ers to pray this prayer as you begin a prayer time together; encourage them to use it as a prayer of their own throughout the day.

Journals

Periodically, your prayer with your group can be devoted to quiet time for the children/youth to reflect and write in their prayer journals.

A journal is really different from a diary. A diary usually seeks to record the events of the day. A journal, on the other hand, attempts to explore the feelings, and perhaps the meanings, behind what is happening.

There are many ways to use journals as prayer; the best way, of course, will be designed by each child/youth as he/she uses the journal. There are many journal-writing starters, which you can suggest:

- At times, you can base the writing topic on the theme currently being studied, for example, "Let's write about a time when we experienced God's forgiveness and the forgiveness of another person."

- Suggest that the children/youth write a dialogue between themselves and Jesus, the Holy Spirit, or a favorite saint. Encourage them to make it a two-way conversation. *What would Jesus say in response to you?*

- Invite them to write a poem using only adjectives about the Eucharist (or some other topic you are studying).

- Encourage your learners to visualize being in their favorite place with Jesus:

  You are alone with Jesus. What is happening? What do you see? What do you hear? Are you saying anything? Is Jesus saying anything?

- Invite them to use their journal to wonder about the four things they would really like to ask God.

- Invite your children/youth to watch for and select a quotation that they especially like. Have them write it in their journal. Talk with God about what it means to them.

- Suggest that they reflect on a recent time they did something for someone else.

  Why did you do it? How did it make you feel? What happened to you because you did it? What will you do in the future because of this experience?

- Invite them to journal about their gifts:

  What do you think are your gifts? What do people tell you are your gifts? Are there other gifts you would like to have? How do you use your gifts? What would you like to say to God about your gifts?"

- Suggest that they journal about their five dreams for the world.

  What would have to happen for those dreams to come true? Is there anything you can do about them?

- Ask them:

  Can you make a list in your journal of seven things for which you are grateful? What can you do because you have these things?

- After reading a Scripture story, invite them to write or draw in their journal what came to mind as they listened.

    Did the story touch your life? What might it mean in today's world, in the time and place where you live?

- Sometimes, simply provide quiet moments so the learners have calm and a prayerful atmosphere to compose their own prayer thoughts.

K k

My niece and her husband enrolled their children for swimming lessons for the first time. Owen (nearly five) loved the water when he was in a motel swimming pool or in a lake during camping trips. (Of course, he had water wings and Mom and Dad.) But the first time he went for swimming lessons, he literally wrapped his arms around his big sister, Abby (almost seven), because he was afraid. The second time, he refused to go into the pool at all.

His solution: He prayed. His sincere, trust-filled prayer was, "God, help me to not be afraid of the water. And please, help me not to sink."

There was no hesitation, no long pondering, no figuring out of what to do. Owen knew what he needed to do: Ask God's help. This was bigger than him, and God would help him.

Owen also knew that nothing was unimportant to God; there's not a dividing line between the sacred and the "secular." Everything is holy; everything belongs to our life, our faith life. Everything is one.

Owen's prayer is ours — for many occasions. How many times can we each pray, "Loving God, help me to not be fearful of _____ . And please, help me not to sink."

- ► When was the last time you thought of going immediately to God?

- ► Do you ever put a dividing line between parts of your life? Are some things "holier" than others?

- ► Would Owen's prayer be helpful to you sometimes?

Kiss of Peace

Including the rituals of our liturgical prayer in our learners' prayer experiences is helpful, making the rituals more comfortable and understandable for them.

In addition to including the Sign of Peace within prayer services, as the children/youth leave at the end of the session, invite them to exchange with you and one another the Sign of Peace. This prayer experience itself provides important moments of personal contact between you and your learners.

L l

A little boy once said to his mother, "Mom, listen to me, but this time with your eyes."

- ▶ Is the prayer of listening easy for me?

- ▶ How do I "listen" to God and the many ways of God's presence? Do I use more than my ears?

- ▶ How am I leading the children, the youth, their families to a prayer of listening?

Labyrinth

The labyrinth has a history that can be traced back more than 4,000 years. The earliest examples, found carved on rocks, all have the same design—the classical labyrinth symbol. Perhaps the most famous labyrinth is the one in Chartres Cathedral in Paris, probably constructed between 1215 and 1221.

More labyrinths have been built in recent years than at any time in the past. The labyrinth is being used by many people, for many reasons, but especially as a contemplative and spiritual tool.

Children and youth respond to the labyrinth because it has the potential to be multi-faceted:

- • It appeals to each person uniquely, and in different ways.

- In the midst of a busy, noisy world, it provides a place, a method for slowing down.

- A walking prayer is a wonderful alternative for many children, especially those who don't want more words.

- Children's creative, imaginative spirits easily find God everywhere.

The main "rule" for a labyrinth is that there is no right or wrong way to walk and pray it. Because of its resurgence in popularity, there are many books and websites with ideas and suggestions on ways to pray the labyrinth. They can be very helpful, but nothing is right or wrong (as with all prayer). Adults often tend to be very serious and somber praying the labyrinth. If children pray it joyfully and that is meaningful for them, who are we to say it's not prayer?

A helpful website about labyrinths, with ideas how labyrinths are used in churches as well as ideas for children (but not specifically prayer ideas), can be found online at www.labyrinthsociety.org.

Lectio divina

Lectio divina (spiritual or divine reading) is an ancient form of prayer in the Church, a way of reading Scripture that invites us to move the words of Scripture into our everyday lives.

Some people will say there are four steps; others will say there are five. Others will say that the fifth step is a given—it pervades everything and all we do.

The first step, *lectio*, is reading the Scripture passage. In the catechetical setting, this is best done aloud, with children/youth reading the passage, reading it creatively. Ask each child/youth to share with the others in his/her small group (without explaining anything): What one word, phrase, or image touched you, stayed with you, struck you, stood out for you?

Meditatio (meditation), the second step, helps the pray-er to connect the passage to his or her life. In the catechetical setting, this step—with children/youth—could be talked about, journaled, or acted out. Where am I in the story? What's the message or meaning of the word, phrase, or image that I chose? How can it be a part of my everyday life? Invite the children, within their small groups, to tell each other why they chose their word, phrase, or image. What does it have to do with their lives?

The third step is *oratio* (prayer). Invite children/youth to be open to God with their gratitude, their needs. With their word, phrase, or image in the background, allow sufficient quiet time for children to talk with God. Then invite prayers of gratitude and petition to be shared within this learning community of young people gathered around God's word.

Contemplatio (contemplation) is the last traditional step. This is an opportunity to do nothing—just to rest and enjoy being in the presence of God. Children/youth can easily be led in this step; they are eager to embrace the gift and wonder of the presence of God.

The fifth step is *actio* (action), which compels us to do something concrete in our everyday lives because of the Scriptural message that has touched our hearts. Invite the children/youth to return to the word, phrase, or image that touched them. Encourage them to share within their groups what this word, phrase, or image is asking them (as individuals) to become—or do—this week. What might it be asking the group as a whole to do this week, or in the days to come?

LEGO prayer

This idea for prayer is adapted from an idea found in *Games for the Soul: Forty Playful Ways to Find Fun and Fulfillment in a Stressful World* by Drew Leder (Hyperion, 1998).

Let each child/youth choose a LEGO block. With that in front of them, invite them to reflect with you as you lead them through:

L represents loved ones. Who are the people to whom you are closest, those whom you love and who love you? Pray for them.

E stands for enemies. Consider your "enemies." Pray for them. As you consider this prayer thought, you might reflect with your young pray-ers what the word "enemy" means. Here are some various ways to think about it:

- Perhaps our goal is to see no one as an enemy.
- Perhaps "enemies" means people we are separated from because of a disagreement, and our purpose is always reconciliation.
- Could an enemy be "a person whose story we have not heard"? If we really knew another person, would we see that we're all in this together?

G represents those in need of guidance and grace. They might be people we know, or people whose positions or jobs need God's help. Pray for them.

O stands for ourselves. Spend some time praying for yourself.

Invite the children/youth to put into writing a prayer that comes to their hearts as they reflect on this LEGO way of praying. Some may choose to focus on just one letter at this time; others may write a prayer incorporating all the areas of focus.

"Let's pretend" prayers

Read a gospel story. Say to your young learners: "Let's pretend we are the people Jesus fed. What would you say? What would our prayers be if we were the people who were just fed?"

Prayer of listening

Mark Twain is known to have said that we have two ears and one mouth and we should use them roughly in that proportion. Meditation and contemplative prayer are certainly prayers of listening, but simple listening prayers can be incorporated in various ways throughout our day, interspersed throughout our catechetical sessions, as well as within our times of community prayer.

Another type of listening prayer is to invite our children/ youth to be attuned to the sounds around them and to then form prayers, flowing from those everyday situations. For instance, when they hear an airplane overhead, encourage them to think about the pilots, the flight attendants, the various people who might be on board. Where might they be going? Why? Pray for them.

Letter to God

If the children's/youth's best friend moved away, wouldn't they want to keep in contact? If a favorite aunt or uncle was out of town or out of the country for a while, wouldn't they want to write to them (via letter, e-mail, or text)?

Encourage your young learners during a prayer service, or a quiet prayer time, to put their thoughts to God on paper—just for themselves and God.

List God's surprises

There is a book, *The God of Surprises* by Gerard W. Hughes, SJ, originally written in 1985, now in its third printing, that has sold more than 250,000 copies. Invite your children/youth to think of all the surprises God has created, all the things that have been surprises in their lives. Ask them to weave these thoughts into a prayer.

Litanies

Litanies, having been part of our Church tradition for a long time, are prayers composed of a series of invocations or intercessions, alternating with brief responses. In group prayer, a litany alternates between a leader and the rest of the people.

Psalm 136, with its repeated refrain ("for God's steadfast love endures forever") is an ancient biblical litany. The "Lord, have mercy," the General Intercessions, and the Lamb of God are forms of litanies in our eucharistic liturgy.

The Litany of the Blessed Virgin (the Litany of Loreto) is a popular litany for Catholics. There are six litanies approved by the Church for public recitation: In addition to the Litany of Loreto, they are the Litany of the Saints, the Litany of the Holy Name of Jesus, the Litany of the Sacred Heart of Jesus, the Litany of the Most Precious Blood of Jesus, and the Litany of Saint Joseph. There are, of course, numerous others that are used for private prayer, and many continue to be composed all the time.

Introduce your children to some of the litanies that are found in the prayer life of the church. Use the prayer form of the litany for your group to compose their own prayers: prayers of thanks, prayers of sorrow, prayers for special needs, prayers around special themes (e.g., Bread of Life Litany, Litany of Thanksgiving, Litany for Peace), etc.

Pray the Litany of Saints

The Litany of the Saints is the oldest litany we possess and is the model for all other litanies. Its first recorded use was in 590 when the pope, Saint Gregory the Great, prescribed its usage for a public procession of thanksgiving. This litany is a call to remember those who have gone before us and to ask their intercession.

This litany is most prominently sung during the Easter Vigil at the beginning of the sacraments of initiation for those to be received that night into the Church, and in the liturgy for holy orders.

Pray the Litany of the Saints; invite your learners to write a Litany of the Saints, incorporating the saints with whom they are most familiar, their patron saints, etc.

Liturgical prayer

Older children and youth, in particular, can be encouraged to express their prayers in the style of our liturgical prayer, using this important structure from our liturgy:

- Greeting—e.g., "God of Compassion…"

- Remember (recalling an attribute of God or one of God's saving acts)—e.g., "You, who always watch over your people…"

- Request—e.g., "Give us your strength and courage…"

- Reason—e.g., "for right now it seems there are times we get scared,"

- Conclusion—e.g., "We ask this through our Lord Jesus Christ, your Son, who lives and reigns with you and the Holy Spirit, God forever and ever. Amen."

Liturgy of the Hours for children

Next to our celebration of liturgy, Liturgy of the Hours is the prayer of the Church that gathers people liturgically throughout the world and "is so arranged that the whole course of the day and night is made holy by the praises of God" (*Constitution on the Sacred Liturgy*, 84). There are many roles within this prayer, which calls forth the gifts of your children/youth: leader, cantor, lector, prayer leader.

The prayer, which is filled with ritual actions and many forms of prayer, prepares children/youth for deepening prayer and for participation in liturgy: singing, silence, candles, the Sign of the Cross, sprinkling with holy water, lighting incense, and bowing at a doxology (the Glory be to the Father).

For more information on Liturgy of the Hours, see *Liturgy of the Hours: Preparing Morning and Evening Prayer* by James Richards (Collegeville: Liturgical Press); *Morning and Evening: A Parish Celebration* by Joyce Ann Zimmerman, CPPS (Chicago: Liturgy Training Publications); and *Catholic Household Blessings and Prayers* (USCCB Publications). A book of prayer for catechists to use with children and young people is *Children's Daily Prayer for the School Year* (Chicago: Liturgy Training Publications).

Liturgy next Sunday

All prayer culminates in our community celebration of liturgy each weekend. To help your learners approach this celebration more prayerfully:

- Invite them to find the common thread that binds the Sunday readings together.

- Have them pretend they are going to give Sunday's homily. From the readings, what would be their topic, their message?

- Take one or two of the prayers in the liturgy and invite them to rewrite them, explaining them or their meaning to the others.

- Pray one of the Scripture readings, using lectio divina.

"Lord, have mercy" prayers

"Lord, have mercy," of course, comes from our liturgical celebration. The biblical roots of this prayer first appear in 1 Chronicles 16:34: "Give thanks unto the Lord; for he is good; for his mercy endures forever."

This scriptural foundation gives us the key to fully understanding the prayer. The prayer "Lord, have mercy" is simultaneously a petition and a prayer of thanksgiving, an acknowledgment of what God has done, what God is doing, and what God will continue to do.

Sometimes when we pray this prayer, we tend to concentrate upon our sinfulness, but it is a prayer of God's mercy, a prayer about the unbelievable, incomprehensible mercy, compassion, and benevolence of our God.

Invite your children/youth to pray this prayer, concentrating upon God's incomparable love rather than their failings.

M m

A young girl told her mother, "I can't wait to get to heaven because they have such beautiful clothes there."

"Honey, where did you get that idea?" her mother asked.

The little girl, having just heard the prayer known as the Memorare, replied, "Mom, remember when we prayed 'to thee do we send up our size (sighs)…'"

> ▶ What would it be like to have such absolute trust when we pray?
>
> ▶ What do you think heaven will be like?

Magnificat

After studying Mary's prayer when she visited her cousin Elizabeth, her prayer in praise of God's work, her Magnificat, invite the children/youth to reflect on their lives. How has God worked in their lives? What has God done for them? Invite them to write a prayer about their lives, using the format of Mary's prayer:

God has done great things for me.

God has _____ .

God has _____ _____ .

God has _____ .

Holy is God's name.

Mandalas

The word "mandala" means circle or wheel in Sanskrit, a sacred circle with a centerpoint. Mandalas have been used for centuries by various cultures as sacred and meditational art forms.

Catholic rose windows, such as those in the Cathedral of Notre Dame, are a form of mandala, created to shine light into a church or cathedral to instill in the viewer the beauty and love of God. The Celtic cross, the crown of thorns, and the labyrinth are other forms of the mandala. Blessed Hildegard von Bingen created many beautiful mandalas to express her visions and beliefs.

Mandalas can be used for prayer in several ways. Three of the many possibilities are:

- Use an existing mandala for meditation, a window into God's love, into the beauty and interdependence of creation. Lead children/youth through a quiet reflection, inviting each to see new connections, to appreciate our unity and wholeness, and to give thanks to God for wonder and gifts.

- Provide children/youth with paper, pencils, crayons, pastels, markers, and paints, and invite them to make their own mandala. You might leave them free to use whatever theme and designs or symbols they wish to use for this mandala of prayer. You might suggest that they create a mandala of prayer focused on a given theme, such as: thanksgiving, creation, forgiveness, hope, faithfulness, discipleship, confirmation, etc.

- Create a group mandala. After your group has studied and reflected on a specific theme together, conclude that unit with a group mandala. Invite each child/youth to create an individual mandala, then bring them together for a much larger unity. One of the lessons of this project, of course, is the realization that everyone has something to offer, each person is an important and integral part of God's family. For some ideas of working with children/youth to create a group mandala (not the prayer part of it, however), visit: www.mandalaproject.org/What/Index.html.

Meditation

Meditation is a prayer form in which we quiet our bodies and minds so that we might open our hearts to God, to the Holy Spirit. In today's noisy and busy world, children and young people—once they are introduced to ways of meditation—find themselves eager to use it, knowing they want and need quiet, slowing-down times to be with God.

There are many approaches and methods for meditation. Use different ones. Introduce various ones to your young learners so they have a variety to choose from, selecting those that are best for them.

Invite the children/youth to find a comfortable position. Sitting straight with their feet on the floor is preferable. Invite them to close their eyes and concentrate for a few moments on quieting their bodies, breathing slowly and deeply. Ask them to become aware of their breathing.

You might wish to begin the meditation by inviting the children to think of a short prayer or prayer phrase, such as "My Lord and my God" or "The Lord is my shepherd" or "Holy, holy God," and repeat the phrase slowly over and over again.

This might encompass the meditation time itself, similar to centering prayer. There are, of course, many methods suggested for meditation.

One helpful method is to suggest that children/youth visualize being with Jesus, and to invite them to talk with him and/or listen to him. You might direct this even further by focusing the topic of conversation around your session's theme, something that has been happening in the lives of your learners, or in current events.

Many adults throughout the world are using Sacred Space at their computers (www.sacredspace.ie) for a few moments of meditation. The creators of Sacred Space also have a space for youth: Sacred Gateway (www.sacredgateway.org), where youth are invited to spend ten minutes praying at their computers with the help of onscreen guidance and Scripture chosen specifically for each day.

The Memorare

The Memorare is one of the Church's traditional prayers that reminds us that we have an advocate and protector in the mother of Jesus, the Blessed Virgin Mary,

The actual author of the Memorare is unknown. It has been traditionally attributed to Saint Bernard of Clairvaux, from the twelfth century. This is possibly because it was championed by another Bernard, the French priest Claude Bernard, who used it extensively in his ministry to the poor and to prisoners in the seventeenth century.

Claude Bernard prayed the Memorare when he was seriously ill. He had some 200,000 copies of the prayer printed and distributed in leaflets in various languages during his lifetime. (In the days before desktop publishing, Kinko's, and the Internet, this was quite an undertaking!)

Music

Praying with music and song, of course, is paramount within our tradition. "When we sing, we pray twice" is an often-quoted saying, attributed to Saint Augustine.

How we use music in prayer is limited only by our creativity and imagination.

- Use the vast repertoire of our liturgical music.

- Use quiet reflective music as a background to readings and for meditation.

- Invite children/youth to put their original prayers to music (their own music or a traditional melody).

- Use rhythm band instruments. Make your own rhythm band instruments.

- Invite children/youth to create PowerPoints of visuals and music to portray their beliefs or feelings.

- Pray for people in different parts of the world through listening to their music. Doodle while listening, while praying. What does your doodle-prayer say to you?

In addition to our inspiring and reflective liturgical and religious music, it is also very possible that some contemporary music puts us in touch with God and our intimate relationship, helps us reflect on our call to be disciples, and calls us to growth and conversion. For instance, with the song "You Raise Me Up," youth can be invited to listen and think about the people in their lives who have raised them up, as well as God, who has always raised them up because of the gift of God's constant presence, grace, and love.

N n

In a small rural parish, during midmorning prayers, the pastor noticed an older man in the first pew. He had no prayer book or rosary, and his head was not bowed, but he seemed very intent – with a large smile on his face. Often he nodded and sometimes laughed out loud!

About an hour later, the pastor was working outside the church as the gentleman was leaving. Father said to him, "It was nice to see you here, laughing in there."

The man smiled and replied, "I was telling the Lord some jokes. It seems like people always tell him all the troubles of the world – and that's OK! – but I think once in a while he needs a good laugh."

► Are there only certain things you talk with God about?

► When is it easier to go to God, in trouble or in happy times?

Name prayer

A name prayer is one in which each letter of a person's name is used as the initial letter for one or more words in a line of prayer. Invite your children/youth to write a name prayer for their own name, a friend's name, or the name of one of their parents. An example would be:

Jesus,
Instill in me a
Love for all
Living creatures

Another way of praying a name prayer is to use a name for God, such as Lord, Jesus, Holy Spirit, Creator God, and invite your learners to choose for each letter a phrase that describes who God is, thus writing a prayer to our Loving God.

L Loving God, you **L**ead us in our life.

O Your love **O**verflows and surrounds us continually and constantly.

R You **R**ejoice over your creation, the work of your hands.

D You give us our **D**aily bread, your constant presence and protection.

Naming the days

"You have got to own your days and name them, each one of them, every one of them, or else the years go right by and none of them belong to you" (from the play *A Thousand Clowns* by Herb Gardner).

Rooting our days, connecting our days to our heritage, our history, gives us—and our children/youth—a wonderful sense of who we are, our tradition, and our interrelatedness. Our liturgical calendar of the saints' days is first and foremost in this. In addition, there are the multitude of cultural celebrations, historical anniversaries, and national and international observances which provide occasions and reasons for our prayer.

Some helpful sites: www.spiritualityandpractice.com/days and www.prayingeachday.org/reflect.html.

Praying in and with nature

Where did Jesus pray? In the gospels, we read more about Jesus praying by the sea, on a mountain, in a garden, or in a field than praying in the synagogue.

Are there times you can move outside for prayer?

Incorporate prayers that celebrate creation, such as Saint Francis of Assisi's Canticle of the Creatures.

Many of the psalms were hymns of praise for the gifts of creation. After your young learners have spent some time outside and perused some psalms (8; 104; 136:1–9; 145; 148), invite them to write their own psalm in praise and thanks for creation.

Today we have many recordings of nature sounds. At times, use those as background to prayer: a spring rain, sounds of dolphins, sounds of rainforests. Invite your learners to careful listening, giving thanks for their part in a vast creation, the part of each created thing in God's universe.

Haiku, a popular form of poetry from Japan, consists of three lines with a syllabic pattern of 5-7-5. Although traditional haiku are often about nature or the changing seasons, they nonetheless manage to convey emotion. With just a few words, they call attention to an observation and, in effect, say, "Look at this," or "Think about this." If they're well written, we can't help but do just that. The haiku calls the reader's attention to the story behind the observation.

Some teachers think children should always be taught to write haiku that follow the 5-7-5 specifications; others disagree, because they feel that the essence of a haiku is the way it describes natural phenomena in the fewest number of words, making an indelible impression on the reader. The effect, they say, is much more important than the number of syllables.

For prayer, that would definitely be true! So introduce your children/youth to haiku (they probably already know the form). Invite them to use it to express a reflection or prayer about the wonder of our natural world.

Invite them to recall what they have seen or experienced when they have been on a nature hike, outdoors at recess, looking at nature photography, playing outside at home, etc. Have them write down their observations. Then, suggest that they find two images that create a striking impression when connected and write them down. Now they need to pare the sentence down so it still describes the scene while inviting the reader to marvel at nature, which is a magnificent way of praying, praising our Creator.

Be mindful during prayer of our call to care for creation, of the current needs of our world regarding the sustainability of our earth. See:

- Catholic Climate Covenant
  catholicclimatecovenant.org/the-st-francis-pledge

- The National Religious Partnership for the Environment
  www.nrpe.org

- Bullfrog Films
  www.bullfrogfilms.com

Newspaper prayers

Our learners today are very aware of the stories that are in the headlines. Bring to your sessions some newspaper stories that show our need for prayer. Placed on a prayer bulletin board, these can provide the basis of a litany of petitions. Praying with these issues as a backdrop helps to form our young people within our rich tradition of Catholic social teaching based on peace and justice. They gradually realize that prayer of petition is not just all about me and what I want, but about being concerned for — being one with — the wider community.

Another way to use newspapers (or Internet news) is to invite young people to read and ponder an article, picture, cartoon, ad, editorial, etc. Suggest that as they reflect on what they have read or seen, they also consider what it has to say about their own lives. Then, they can write a short prayer expressing their thoughts and feelings.

A slight variation of this is to invite the children/youth to pretend that they are the person who is currently in the news. As that person, they can write a prayer (thanksgiving, praise, sorrow, or petition) which that person might pray.

O o

A mom took her son to their pastor. "Father," she said, "would you please listen to Tyler say the Our Father? He's got it all mixed up."

So the pastor listened and asked him to say the Our Father.

"Our Father, who art in New Haven, how do you know my name?" Tyler began.

"Well," said the mother, when the two returned. "Did you straighten him out?"

"No," said the pastor. "I wouldn't change a word of the way he says the Our Father. His way shows that he understands two important things about God: First, that God is very near; second, that God knows him personally."

▶ When do I feel God near?

▶ When do I hear God call me by name?

O Antiphons

These rich prayers, prayed during the Octave before Christmas, December 17–23, have been part of our liturgical tradition since the very early Church. Each one highlights a title for the Messiah: O Wisdom, O Lord, O Root of Jesse, O Key of David, O Rising

Sun, O King of the Nations, and O Emmanuel. Each one also refers to the prophecy of Isaiah of the coming of the Messiah.

During this Octave, these prayers/prophesies can be prayed, reflected upon and studied with their related scriptural readings and prayers, artistically portrayed (as they have been by many artists) and compared to the hymn, "O Come, O Come Emmanuel." Each verse of this well-known hymn parallels one of the antiphons.

Another prayerful experience for children/youth is to create their own—similar—O Antiphons for each season, or liturgical season, of the year (e.g., fall, spring, Lent, Easter).

Our Father

This prayer, found in Luke (11:2–4) and Matthew (6:9–13), sums up what we believe in and hope for. It consists of an address (Our Father) and two sets of petitions. The first set focuses on the action of God as Father and the coming of God's kingdom. The second set focuses on our needs and fears as they are met by the action of God. For a deep explanation and interpretation of the Our Father, see the *Catechism of the Catholic Church* (#2759–2865).

Because this prayer is so pivotal, there are many ways to use it creatively in prayer and reflection, to help our learners deepen their appreciation, love, and understanding of it.

- Invite your learners to make an Our Father booklet. Devote a page to each phrase of the prayer. Taking a page a week (don't rush through it), the children/youth can use drawings, paint, abstract art, poetry, symbols, prayerful reflections, newspaper stories, etc., to illustrate the meaning of each line (e.g., for "hallowed be thy name"—paste the word "God" in bright gold or colored paper; for "give us this day our daily bread"—find magazine pictures of all the things we need for life each day).

- Have the children/youth look up and then reflect on various Scripture passages, which deepen the message of each line of the Our Father, for instance:

    Our Father   *Isaiah 6:3*

    Who art in heaven   *Acts 17:28*

    Hallowed be thy name   *Romans 14:11; 1 Corinthians 6:11*

    Thy Kingdom come   *2 Peter 3:13*

    Thy will be done on earth as it is in heaven
        John 15:17; Romans 12:2; Matthew 7:21

    Give us this day our daily bread   *Luke 12:29*

    Forgive us our trespasses as we forgive those who
        trespass against us   *Luke 17:4*

    And lead us not into temptation but deliver us from evil
        Ephesians 5:8–21

    For thine is the Kingdom   *Colossians 1:20*

    and the power   *1 Corinthians 1:25*

    and the glory forever. Amen.   *Revelation 4:8, 11*

- Invite the children/youth to take a disposable camera and go on a month-long search (during their days at school, in their neighborhoods, with their families, etc.) to take pictures of situations that illustrate each line of the Our Father.

- Encourage the children/youth to work together in small groups to write an extended version of the Our Father. (Each group might want to work on one phrase.) For example:

Our Father…

>…our God who loves us very much

>…our God who is the Giver of Life

>…Gentle Goodness

>…Creator of all that is

Who art in heaven…

>…who walks the earth with us

>…who carries us when we fall

>…who is with the sick, the poor, the dying, the suffering

>…who is in Iraq, Afghanistan, Haiti

- Saint Ignatius suggested to those seeking to grow in prayer to pray the Our Father very slowly and silently in harmony with the pattern of deep, relaxing breathing. Invite children/youth to pray only one word with each slow breath, letting the mind, heart, and imagination dwell on that single word.

- Saint Ignatius also suggested a second method: Become relaxed and dwell on the first word of the Our Father for as long as it is meaningful. Then, move on to the second word. (A young novice once asked Saint Teresa of Avila, "Mother, what shall I do to become a contemplative?" Without missing a beat, Teresa responded, "Say the Our Father—but take an hour to say it.") Lead the children/youth in a quiet prayer time that gives them the freedom and space to pray in this way.

- Throughout our history, the Our Father has been put to music in various settings. Locate as many as you can. Use these to frequently pray the Our Father through song.

- Pray the Our Father with gestures. Children/youth could design their own gestures, or you could teach a set of gestures. You could also use American Sign Language, Native American signs, or simple dance motions.

- Invite the children/youth to create napkin rings for members of their families with a phrase from the Our Father printed on them. (The prayer can be run off on mailing labels.)

- Create a bulletin board with newspaper, magazine, and Internet articles that depict the various lines of the Our Father.

- Make a prayer cloth for your prayer table using fabric crayons. Have children/youth write the lines of the Our Father around the edges of the prayer cloth.

- Since praying the Our Father can easily become routine, use only one line of the prayer at a time. Following each portion of the Our Father, invite your learners to compose a litany based on its meaning. For instance, following "forgive us our trespasses," they might compose a litany of forgiveness.

- There is a building in the Holy Land that contains sixty large plaques, each one showing the Our Father in a different language. Invite your children/youth to learn the Our Father in another language. If a parent speaks another language, invite him/her into your group to teach the children/youth the Our Father.

- Help children/youth to imagine as many ways as possible to live the Our Father in their daily lives. They can do this phrase by phrase, for example:

*Give us this day our daily bread…*rely on God; don't worry; talk to God about the things we need; always give thanks; help those who are hungry.

*Forgive us our trespasses…*pray the Act of Contrition; ask for forgiveness; forgive others; don't hold grudges.

Others' prayers

Encourage your young pray-ers to watch for prayers from others that they like, with which they identify, that they would like to use. Invite them to copy them into their journals, or make them into bookmarks so they have them handy in order to use them often.

This one, written by John Henry Cardinal Newman (1801–1890), an English church leader, might be one example:

Jesus, shine through me and be so in me that every person
I come in contact with may feel your presence in my soul.
Amen.

One that I always carry in my calendar comes from Fr. Mychal Judge, a Franciscan priest, chaplain of the Fire Department of New York. He was one of the first recorded victims of the September 11, 2001, attacks. People who knew and ministered with him say he was accustomed to handing out cards with this prayer:

Lord, take me where you want me to go. Let me meet who
you want me to meet. Tell me what you want me to say,
and keep me out of your way.

P p

A story is told of a workman who took a break and read a book of psalms. His employer approached him and inquired: "Why are you reading all of a sudden, right in the middle of your work activity?"

The man replied, "It doesn't seem to bother anyone that in the middle of praying I am thinking about work. Why is it that in the middle of work I can't think for a minute or two about prayer?"

▶ Do moments of prayer pervade my day?

▶ As a catechist, how can I help the children/ youth grow in their understanding and practice of integrating prayer continually — not just at "designated times"?

Paper prayers

Each person has three sheets of paper: white, blue, and green. Invite them: "On the blue paper, write things you're thankful for. On the green paper, list things you're sorry for or would like to change in your life. On the white paper, jot down some worries or concerns you have right now. Don't write your name down."

After the children/youth have finished writing, collect all the papers, putting them in stacks according to color. Then invite your learners to count off one, two, and three. All the ones go to the blue pile, the twos to the green pile, the threes to the white pile.

The directions now are: "Take one of the papers in your pile, then find a person from each of the other groups to form a trio. You need to have a one, two, and three in your group."

After the new groups are formed: "Now you can pray for the things on your papers. Thank God for the things on your blue paper; ask God to help us change in the ways listed on the green paper; ask for God's peace for the things on the white paper. Be sure each person in your trio gets to pray."

Partner prayer

This partner prayer is prayed with your children/youth in groups of two. Sometimes when we pray, we have the tendency to close our eyes, or "cast our eyes down." For some types of prayer, that is probably very appropriate. Yet, for other types, perhaps it is very important that we are aware of the community with whom we are praying. This prayer encourages and promotes that!

The two prayer partners face each other, because there are also gestures that accompany the words. Before beginning the prayer, too, it would be advantageous to reflect with the children/youth about praying together as a community, recognizing the people with whom we are praying. This prayer gives us the opportunity to look at another person, remembering that this person is a special, unique person created and totally loved by God.

I am the Body of Christ.
(hands reverently pointing to self)

You are the Body of Christ.
   (hands reverently pointing toward your partner)

Together we are one in the Spirit,
   (partners join hands)

Because our Loving God lives in us.
   (partners raise joined hands)

This prayer can be incorporated into a prayer service or can stand alone as an opening or closing prayer, or an anytime prayer. It might be used at a time when everyone needs to be reminded of their unity.

Another alternative would be to pray it once, then take a moment of silence or peaceful music, then pray it a second time with a different partner.

Peace prayers

Since at any given moment, there are, unfortunately, numerous wars going on throughout the world, not to mention other types of violence, perhaps we should include prayer and reflection on peace frequently in our prayer time. Here are a few—among many—possibilities:

- During prayer, invite the children/youth to reflect on their image of God. How do they pray to God during times when people are especially concentrated upon war and violence? Is our God a God who helps us fight wars or a God of peace? A God of retaliation or a God of unconditional love for every human being? Is God non-violent? Take time to ponder these questions during prayer time.

- Pretend you are president of the Peaceable Kingdom. What laws would govern your land?

- Do a Scripture search on the word "peace." What does God's word tell us about being people of peace?

- Have a New Year's Broom of Peace Ritual. Using a new broom, pray: "Loving God, who makes all things new, help us to be new creations. New Year's Broom of Peace, sweep clean our meeting place of the old year's grudges, mistakes, and unkindness." (Symbolically sweep several times across the threshold. Close the door as you gather in a circle. The broom is slowly passed from one to another.) "New Year's Broom, sweep from all hearts fear and hurt memories. May our hearts, now swept clean, have room for peaceful new beginnings. With peace in our hearts, may we spread the Peace of God to all we meet in this new year." (You may want to give this ritual prayer to your children/youth to take home to do as a family prayer.)

- Visit the World Peace Prayer Society (www.worldpeace. org).

Photo praying

The possibilities with photo prayers are, of course, endless; let your creativity unfold and you'll find countless opportunities for remembering people in prayer.

Invite your children/youth to bring to your session a photo of one or several persons they would like to remember in prayer. These photos, then, become the spring board of storytelling, remembering, and heartfelt prayer, gathered together in community in your prayer space, such as:

> "This is my niece, my sister's six-month-old baby, Maria, who just had surgery and needs our prayers to continue to be strong and healthy."

"My picture is of my great-grandfather. He died before I was born, so I never knew him, but my mom and dad tell me stories about him all the time. He was kind, loved his family, and always looked for ways to help people. I pray all the time that I can be like him. Perhaps we can pray today that all of us can be people like him, wherever we are."

"This is the family that used to live down the street from us, the Clarks. Kevin was my best friend. They moved away to another state. We miss all of them because they were wonderful neighbors. I pray for the Clarks and thank God for people who are good neighbors, great friends in our lives."

The photos can also evoke memories of the events that are captured, or the nature that this portrayed, or the world that is represented. What would your children/youth want to pray? Would there be prayers of praise, thanksgiving, petition?

As your young learners reminisce about the photo(s) they brought, what do they see happening? How does it make them feel? For what, then, do they wish to pray?

Picture praying

Show the children/youth a picture (from a magazine, the Internet, an art piece, a newspaper, etc.). Invite them to reflect on it. What is happening? What might the people be feeling? What does it remind them of in their own lives? What does it tell them about God? Invite them to write a prayer based on their thoughts and feelings that were evoked by the picture.

Pilgrimage

Throughout our Catholic history, we have a rich spiritual tradition of making pilgrimages to holy places. You can build on this tradition—and relate it to everyday life—by inviting your children/youth to go on a pilgrimage together to celebrate a Marian feast (this idea can be adapted for other feasts and other occasions).

Lead your children/youth to a spot on the parish grounds or near the meeting place for your catechetical session. Try not to use the church building, and do not tell your "pilgrims" their destination. (The reasons for these two cautions for your pilgrimage will soon become clear.)

Recall with your "pilgrims" Mary's journeys: her visit to her cousin Elizabeth, her journey to Bethlehem, the flight to Egypt with Joseph and the infant Jesus, traveling with Joseph and Jesus to the Temple in Jerusalem when Jesus was twelve years old, following Jesus on the road to Calvary, rushing to the tomb on Easter morning (surely Mary was one of the women).

These were all physical journeys, but Mary made interior journeys as well—from confusion to understanding (Annunciation), from worry (during the journey to the Temple) to relief at finding Jesus; from sorrow (Calvary) to the joy of Easter, etc.

Explain that now you are going to make a pilgrimage together and what will happen on the way. Pray a prayer of blessing together for a safe journey.

Before setting out, divide the group into pairs. Give each pair a 3 x 5 card with the following questions:

- On your life's journey so far, what are some of the gifts God has given you?

- On your life's journey, have you had some difficult times? What has helped you get through these hard times?

- Tell about a time on your life's journey when you really felt God's presence with you.

As they walk on their pilgrimage, the children are asked to share their responses to these questions with their partner, making this pilgrimage a time of storytelling about their faith journey.

Lead the children/youth on a walking pilgrimage through the parish grounds (or if time permits, through the neighborhood and back to the parish grounds), and end up somewhere of your choosing on the parish grounds. It could be in the church, at a grotto, in a garden, in a gathering place, anywhere you choose.

Upon arriving at your destination, lead your pilgrims in this threefold prayerful activity:

- Guided Meditation: Help them to quiet down and reflect upon the thoughts they just shared on their pilgrimage as you lead them through these questions:

  How did you feel about talking with another person about your life's journey?

  Did you discover anything new about yourself?

  Did you discover anything new about your partner?

  Did you discover something new about your relationship with God?

  Following quiet time for individual reflection on these questions, there can be some sharing within the whole group.

- Group Discussion: Remind the pilgrims that a pilgrimage takes people to a holy place. Ask, "Is this a holy place?" Through discussion and leading questions, try to help the pilgrims understand that wherever this pilgrimage has taken them is a holy place—even if it is not inside the church and may not look "holy." We believe that any place where two or three are gathered in Jesus' name is a holy place, and that all creation is holy and graced.

- Prayer: After sharing a gospel passage highlighting the event in Mary's life which you are celebrating, invite your pilgrims to pray one decade of the rosary based on one of the journeys of Mary; the Visitation, for example, which is celebrated on May 31. Before each Hail Mary, have a different child/youth focus the meditation with a prayer such as:

> *Thank you, Gracious God, for the example of Mary, who journeyed in order to go to help her cousin Elizabeth. Hail Mary….*

> *Help us always to be ready, like Mary, to give a helping hand whenever and wherever it is needed. Hail Mary…*

> *God, who asked Mary to bring Jesus to Elizabeth, use us to bring Jesus to the people we meet each day. Hail Mary…*

> *We thank you, Loving God, for being with us on our journey through life; keep us always aware of the many ways you will be present with us in the future. Hail Mary…*

The pilgrimage ends with the Sign of Peace and a concluding hymn.

Pocket prayer

In olden times, people who were in danger used to sew the words of Psalm 91 into their clothes as a reminder to pray for protection. Invite your children/youth to consider what prayer they would like to keep in their pocket to protect and guide them throughout the day. They might want to pick portions of Psalm 91, choose a prayer that they know by heart, search the psalms or other Scripture for words that comfort them, or make up a prayer of their own. Invite them to write it down, decorate it, and keep it in their pocket.

Praying with poetry

Some of our greatest prayers, of course, are poems. Invite your children/youth into prayer through engaging with poetry in various ways.

Use poetry for prayer and reflection. Take a poem for quiet reflection about God, about life's questions. It does not need to be a specifically "religious" poem. Many poems, from our great poets or by today's authors, adults as well as children, through reflection and quiet times with God, can lead the children/youth to conversation with God about things that matter.

Invite the children/youth to search for poems that speak to them of God. Encourage them to look within the many cultures of our world. These can be gathered together in a large, beautiful journal placed in your group's gathering place.

Invite the children/youth to write their prayers, their thoughts to God, in the form of poetry. Often, using this different medium allows new ideas, new reflections to surface which might not have come through in a less symbolic way.

Popsicle prayer sticks

Using popsicle sticks—or even better, larger tongue depressors— is one visual aid to prayer. Prepare the sticks ahead of time (or have helpers from the parish do it for you, especially some who are good artists). Using stickers or real art, decorate each with a different theme, a different gift from God (food, creation, animals, people, colors, school, the seasons, the night sky, friends, homes, family, etc.). Punch a small hole at one end, threading a piece of long yarn through it, looping it, so that there's a long string attached that makes it easier to handle.

Keep the prayer sticks together in an attractive container, and periodically invite each child to take one and reflect on the gift from God depicted on it. How is that gift alive in the child's life? Invite them to write a prayer of thanks. Then, during a group prayer, invite those who wish to share their prayers.

At times, invite the children to take their individual prayer sticks home for a week, to place in their bedrooms. (With a loop of yarn, the stick can be hung on a doorknob.) This can be the child's "thank you" prayer for the week. After the week is over, the child returns it and perhaps chooses another.

Porch prayers

Suggest to your children/youth that they pray porch prayers with their families. With their family, they can sit on the porch or deck in the backyard, listen quietly for sounds, and then pray short prayers related to the sounds they hear. For instance: As they hear birds singing, they can thank God for music or small creatures. If they hear a siren, they can pray for the safety of those waiting for help.

Prayer chain

A paper chain can be used in countless ways to spark ideas for children/youth as they pray.

A petitionary prayer chain can be a reminder of all those for whom your young learners have promised to pray. They can make a link for each person who has asked for or needs their prayers, adding to the chain as the days and weeks go by. The needs can be generic (the unemployed, those in poverty, those who are sick, those who are grieving, those in countries at war, etc.); or specific needs can be placed on a link (Mrs. Caven who has cancer, our catechumens and candidates, my dad who is looking for a job, the engaged couples of our parish, my uncle who is serving as a Marine, our confirmation candidates, Mr. Jimmet who recently died). As the chain grows throughout the weeks, it will be a visible reminder for the children/youth of our connection as the Body of Christ, our need for one another.

There are numerous ways to build a prayer chain of thanksgiving. One way of deepening young people's gratitude to God, as well as to people, is—for a given period—to invite them to think of people or groups they all know and are grateful for (e.g., the parish council, the police in our community, our pastor, our teachers at school, etc.). As they name these people, they write their name(s) on a link and watch their chain of thanksgiving grow. After a given time, the children/youth take the links off and write a "thank you" note—with a prayer—to the person (or group), telling them how grateful they are for who they are and what they do, and asking God's blessing for them.

Prayer partners

Invite your parishioners to each adopt a child/youth in your parish's catechetical program, and to pray for that young person during the coming catechetical year. The parishioner can be given the first name and grade level of the child/youth for whom the parishioner is praying. Your young person can be given the name (and address, if the person chooses) of the person who is praying. If the parents of the child/youth desire (because they may know the parishioner), the child might send the parishioner a "thank you" note, Christmas card, etc.

A variation of this might be that parishioners "adopt" an entire group from your catechetical program, e.g., Mr. Clark's Monday evening sixth-grade group. With many volunteers from the parish, you might have ten or twelve parishioners praying for each group. The children/youth, in turn, could remember these parishioners in their group prayer, also sending them periodic "thank you" cards—with a prayer—signed by the group.

Prayer of pondering

Encourage the children/youth to choose one word, one phrase, or one line of Sunday's gospel. Give them quiet time to mull it over in their minds and hearts, not analyzing it or studying it, but just pondering it.

Prayer rocks

Invite your children to make prayer rocks. Collect small rocks. Wrap them in brightly colored cloth, tied with yarn or ribbon. Attach to the yarn a card with this poem:

I'm your prayer rock
And this is what I do
Put me on your pillow
Until the day is through.

When you turn back the covers
And climb in for the night,
Whack! I will remind you
To talk with God and shut the light.

After you have prayed
Dump me on the floor,

I'll stay there till the morning
To give you help once more.

Get up in the morning
Crack! You'll stub your toe
To remind you to pray to God
Just before you go.

It's obvious, then, what happens next: Children take them home to keep them in their bedrooms and follow the directions on the card, as a reminder for prayer first thing in the morning and last thing in the evening.

Prayer space

Sometimes we need spaces where it's hard *not* to pray. Everything about these places calls us to prayer.

That's why we need a place—a space—at our meeting site that's set apart, in which the only thing that happens is prayer.

Can this space be large enough to have some quiet empty space surrounding it, so that its importance is emphasized, that it's not just pushed off into a corner or a cluttered area? The space around it might be carpeted and/or have a few pillows or chairs, especially if children/youth are able to come to this area when their other activities are completed.

The covering of the table could be changed to coincide with the liturgical seasons: purple and pink for Advent, different shades of green for Ordinary Time, deep purple for Lent, etc.

The focal point, of course, is the open Scriptures. A candle, representing Jesus, the Light of the World, is also an important must. During Advent, this can be replaced by the Advent wreath.

Depending on the liturgical season—and/or the theme of your session—other symbols could be added to the prayer space: during Lent, palm and ashes; an icon of Mary on her feast day or when you are studying about her; a bowl of water during the Easter season or when you are studying baptism; photos of loved ones on All Souls' Day.

As important as the prayer space is, and as often as it should be used for your planned prayer time, it doesn't mean you can't—or shouldn't—pray in other places. The message we always want to convey is that prayer can happen anytime, anywhere.

Prayer tour

Gather your group together in a van, your parish's bus, etc., and go on a "prayer tour," stopping at different locations within your parish and community. For instance:

- Hospital: Pray for those you know who are sick, those in this hospital, and all who are suffering from illness.

- School: Pray for friends, teachers, people who care and help us to grow.

- Police department: Pray for safety and the peacefulness of the neighborhood.

- In the middle of a neighborhood: Pray for families, for people living alone, for neighbors—and pray that people will always care for each other.

- Funeral home: Pray for those who have died and for those who are grieving.

Prayers from the Church

Invite your learners to pray for one another, and at the same time they will be learning about the structure, format, and wording of some of the prayers we use in our liturgy and sacraments. Gather some prayers from the Sacramentary. Print one prayer each on a 3 x 5 card, so that there's one for each child/youth.

Write into each prayer the name of one of your learners. The cards are then folded and placed in a basket. During prayer time, the basket is passed around and each person takes a card and prays for that person for a given period of time.

Some sample prayers:

> *God, our Creator, may the work and studies of Tyler bring him growth in this life and help extend the Kingdom of God. Through Christ our Lord. Amen.*

> *Gracious God, make Abby aware of Jesus' presence among us and bless her with Christ's grace, mercy, and peace so that she will live in truth and love. Through Christ our Lord. Amen.*

When the time is over, the cards can be given to the person whose name is in the prayer; a new set can be done and the prayer practice done again, with the same prayers and different names or with a new set of prayers.

Praying the psalms

In her book *Undercurrents* (Harper SanFrancisco, 1995), Martha Manning says, "It's incredible to me that we never learned the psalms as children. All that time and energy memorizing the catechism when the real thing was right here. It's like memorizing *TV Guide* rather than watching the show."

In *The Gift of Peace* (Loyola Press, 1997), Joseph Cardinal Bernardin says, "I have found the psalms to be very special because they relate in a very direct, human way the joys and sorrows of life, the virtues, the sins. They convey the message that good ultimately wins out. And as you see the people who are mentioned in the psalms struggling to be united with the Lord, it gives you a certain amount of encouragement, knowing that even thousands of years ago this same thing was happening."

To share the prayerful power of the psalms with our young people is a gift we give them for the rest of their lives. Here are some methods to deepen this prayer within them:

- Invite each child/youth to cover a cereal box with colorful paper and decorations. Throughout your year's exploration and prayer with the psalms, have each write their favorite lines from the psalms on the box. It can then be placed on their family dinner (or breakfast) table.

- Sing "Be still and Know" (Psalm 46:11) to the tune of Amazing Grace:

    Be still and know that I am God.
    Be still and know that I am God.
    Be still and know that I am God.
    Be still, be still, be still.

    Sing the song again, adding sign language. If no one knows sign language, use these simple motions. Put a finger to your lips for "be still," point to your head for "and know," and point to the sky for "I am God."

- Pass around a rock as you read Psalm 18:2–3. Invite each person to share how the rock suggests a worry or concern in his/her life right now. Pass the rock around once again. Encourage them to share ways the rock symbolizes God's comforts and security in the midst of troubles.

- Challenge each person to create a "Where to look in the psalms when you feel…" list. A beginning would be:

    afraid: 3, 4, 27, 46, 49, 56, 81, 118

    confused: 10, 12, 73

    guilty: 19, 32, 38, 51

    happy: 19, 96

    impatient: 13, 27, 37, 40

    jealous: 37

    sorry: 32, 51, 66

    sad: 13

    thankful: 118, 136, 138

    worried: 37

    They could then use this information to make a bookmark for their Bibles.

- The psalms help us discover the attributes of God, such as forgiveness, justice, love, mercy, and power. Have each child/youth look through several psalms and make a list of the characteristics of God. Use these ideas to create an A-to-Z poem of praise. Begin with the words, "God is…" Then for every letter of the alphabet, brainstorm adjectives that describe God.

- Help the children/youth discover some ways of praying the psalms:

    They can pray *with* a psalm, that is, use the psalm as their prayer. They could imagine that they are the psalmist and adopt the words of the psalm as their own prayer.

    They could pray *from* a psalm, that is, use the psalm

as a source of ideas for prayer. Imagine the sort of situation and people that fit the psalm. Pray for these people using some of the words of the psalm. Memorize (or write down) a phrase, line, or verse from the psalm and use it throughout your daily activities as a source for meditation or as a trigger for short spontaneous prayers. Some might want to write, as a prayer to God, a short personal reflection or response to the psalm.

- Invite the children/youth to choose a person currently in the news. What kind of psalm might this person pray? Ask them to find one in the Book of Psalms, then write a modern-day psalm that might come from his/her lips.

- Have each person choose a favorite line from a psalm to be their mantra. (A mantra is a word or phrase that is repeated often, so it runs through your mind as you breathe, work, and play.)

- Invite the children/youth to make a set of dinner placemats for their families. Put a different passage from the psalms on each one.

- Encourage everyone to look through their parish hymnals, finding the hymns their parish uses most often. Which ones are based on psalms?

- Invite the children/youth to put the words of their favorite psalm to music—a well-known melody or their own composition.

- As the various liturgical seasons are celebrated, have your learners work in small groups to search for psalms that would reflect the emotions and feelings of that liturgical season.

- Invite your youth to take a camcorder and/or a flip camera to record visuals to accompany the praying of a psalm.

- Have your group make and decorate a prayer box. Inside put 150 slips of paper, each with a number from 1 through 150. Pull out a different slip each day (or each week); find and pray that psalm.

- Connect a piece of children's literature with one of the psalms. For instance, *The Runaway Bunny* by Margaret Wise Brown tells the beautiful story of a mother rabbit who pursues her little bunny who keeps threatening to run away. In a very believable way, it reminds us of the constant, pursuing presence of our loving God. Likewise, Psalm 139 describes God's presence with us no matter where we may go.

- The Old Testament includes numerous accounts of God's hand leading or guiding people. Many of the most inspirational reminders of God's hand are in the Book of Psalms: Psalms 22; 23; 46; 71:4; 79:8–11; 106; 139:9–10; 142:5; 144:7–8; 145:16. After reading these passages, look through books of Christian symbols to find symbols for "the hand of God." Choose the one that best represents God's presence. Invite everyone to design their own posters with their favorite passages and symbols.

- The most important prayer we pray is that of thanksgiving to our gracious God. Throughout the year, invite your learners to compile a booklet of thanksgiving prayers. Include lines from the psalms: 9:2; 30:5; 34; 52:11; 57:10; 66; 67; 69:31; 75:2; 86:12; 92:2; 95:2; 97:12; 105:1; 106:1; 107;1, 8, 15, 21, 31; 108:4; 111:1; 118:1, 21, 29; 124; 136:1; 138:1–2; 139:14; 147:7; 150:6.

- Encourage everyone to write their own prayer according to the form and structure of the psalms. Have them choose a psalm they especially like. Encourage them to write their prayer with the same number of verses, patterns, and structure.

Prefaces as prayers

The Roman Missal contains many beautiful Prefaces, the beginning of the Eucharistic Prayer. They can be prayed "as is" or easily adapted for use as opening prayers for your catechetical session. Children/youth can recite or sing the "Holy, holy, holy" in response.

Priceless moments

When Abby shouts out, "There's a gigantic blue butterfly outside our window," your natural response might be to ignore her or scold her for disrupting the group. There is a book—*The Geranium on the Window Sill Just Died but Teacher You Went Right On* (by Albert Cullum, Harlin Quist Books, 2000)—which reminds us that what is happening here and now in the life of children/youth is most important. Thus, for a few moments, put aside your lesson plan, and quietly move everyone to the window so they can savor this gift of God's creation.

Create a spontaneous prayer time, thanking God for all the beautiful things in creation, and in their lives.

I learned this lesson well when I was teaching in Las Vegas and one fine day it snowed. It almost never snows in that city. It snows in the mountains, so the children were used to seeing snow on the mountains, but they had never experienced it coming down in their city, outside their windows. Yet, it probably was one of the best prayer times, a time to thank God for the unique, interesting things in creation: falling snow, giraffes with long necks, ants who can build mounds for homes, etc.

Processions

Many catechists begin their sessions with an Enthronement of the Bible in their prayer space, moving to the space in procession.

Processions have been a part of our heritage from the very beginning. After Constantine's legalization of Christianity early in the fourth century, the church began to conduct public, outdoor processions in which images or crosses or other Christian symbols were often carried.

To illustrate the transition from conversation and activity to prayer, rather than having each child/youth moving (skipping, running, etc.) to your prayer space, go in a procession. It will call attention to the reality that this time is now something different: You are entering (and leaving) holy ground, a sacred time and place.

At times it can be done in silence, other times accompanied by music, other times singing or chanting a simple prayer-song. Depending upon the prayer (and the music), you may circle the room several times to make the procession longer.

During the Enthronement of the Bible, the children/youth carry candle(s) and, of course, the Scriptures. At other times, depending upon the time of the year and the theme of the prayer, they might carry other liturgical symbols and/or something they have drawn, made, sculpted, a basket of intentions, etc.

Q q

When my great-nephew, Tyler, was two years old, he was at my apartment near Christmastime. As he was playing with my Nativity set, we were talking about Jesus, especially about Jesus still being with us today.

In the midst of our conversation, I received a phone call. After I hung up, Tyler asked, "Was that Jesus?"

As I reflected on his simple question, I realized how true it was. That's where Christ is today — in each one of us. Christmas isn't just a past event.

▶ Does each prayer time and experience help me deepen my awareness of the closeness of Jesus to me, within my world?

▶ As a catechist, which prayer experiences do I see helping my children/youth most experience the presence of Jesus?

Dear God, thank you for my baby brother, but what I really prayed for was a puppy.

> • JOYCE, WWW.CATHOLICLINKS.ORG/
> CTOSILETTERSTOGOD.HTM,
> ACCESSED AUGUST 1, 2010)

▶ How do we pray prayers of petition (prayers for ourselves)?

- ▶ How often do prayers of thanks follow our prayers of petition?

- ▶ In what ways, with what emphasis, do we teach our children/youth about prayer of petition?

Questions for God

Invite your children/youth to imagine that they have all the time in the world to spend with God. What are the questions they have always wanted to ask?

Then, at times, you might also invite them to reflect on and/or write the answers they think God might give them for their questions. If they were God, what would their answers be?

Quiet time

A few moments of quiet listening is a fruitful way for youngsters to pray. To what are they listening? Depending upon the day, the time, or what might have just happened within your session, their responses to this quiet listening can — and should — change.

Some responses that might bubble up in their quiet listening might be: simply stillness, a favorite sung psalm refrain, a word that comes because of what they've heard during the session, something God might be saying, a sound that might be speaking to them that usually they don't hear, etc.

Prayer quilts

Quilts, of course, are traditionally made from fabric and sewn together, but the "quilting concept" could also be used with other media (e.g., poster board, etc.).

Invite your young pray-ers to depict (in fabric, through drawing, paint, etc.) an image to illustrate a theme about which things your group wishes to remember in prayer, e.g., the meaning of Eucharist, the Spirit in our lives, our response to God in trust, etc.

This, of course, can be a permanent addition to your prayer space and can often be used to initiate prayer.

R r

A father and son were hiking the back trails. The boy stopped to inspect a medium-sized boulder that was partially obstructing the trail.

"Dad, do you think I can move that rock?"

The man carefully looked at the rock and said, "Yes, son, if you use all your strength, you can move that rock."

The boy braced against the rock and pushed and strained with all his might…the rock didn't budge.

"Well, Dad, you were wrong. I can't move that rock."

"No, son, I wasn't wrong. I said that if you used all your strength, you could move that rock. But you didn't use all your strength…because you didn't ask me for help."

▶ Do we use all our strength? Do we go to God in prayer?

▶ Prayer doesn't end, though, in just words. It also includes actions. God has given me the strength, the ability, the courage to do that for which I am praying (e.g., bring peace to my corner of the world, visit those who are sick, etc.). How well am I doing?

When I marched with Martin Luther King in Selma, I felt my legs were praying. • RABBI ABRAHAM HESCHEL

▶ Can actions be prayer? Actions of justice?

▶ When have you felt you were praying through something you did?

Random Acts of Kindness

Random Acts of Kindness has become a movement inspiring people to practice kindness and pass it on to others. There is now the Random Acts of Kindness Foundation (www.randomactsof-kindness.org), whose aim is to help people create a better world by spreading awareness and increasing engagement in kind actions.

We can bring this practice to prayer. Create prayers of thanks for the many kindnesses that the children/youth have experienced, helping them to be more aware of the countless ways that people care about them and for them all the time.

Ask God's help that during the coming week, they might always be awake and aware of people's needs, and attuned to ways they can be agents of random acts of kindness, making their world a brighter place. Who is or could be the patron saint of random acts of kindness?

Prayer of reaching out

This idea could go on and on, as our children/youth respond to their baptismal call to be involved in justice and service constantly. Our call to prayer is only one part of our call; it never ends there. We know there's always a second part: service — to be the Body of Christ in our world, to wash feet in service as Jesus did at the Last Supper.

Prayer enables us to respond in service. At the same time, connect prayer to outreach in as many ways as you can.

For instance, invite your children/youth to participate in your parish's food drive. In addition to earning the money to purchase the canned goods, have them compose a prayer of blessing and tape it to each can. These gifts—before they are given to the needy—can be part of the Presentation of Gifts during the liturgy. Liturgical guidelines say that in addition to the gifts of bread and wine, gifts for the poor are the other elements that may be a part of the Presentation of Gifts.

Reflective prayer after reaching out is another prayer not to be missed. Reaching out to others is crucial, but what has happened to me? Lead the children/youth through a reflective prayer—and sharing in small groups—to help them prayerfully consider the impact upon them.

Begin with a Scripture passage of God's call to each of us to be a person for others. Ask questions, such as: Did you learn something new about yourself, emotionally? socially? intellectually? spiritually? Was this service necessary? Why? Do you see the poor, hungry, homeless, etc., differently? If yes, how? Has the way you look at the world been affected? Do you see more connections, concerns, conflicts? If so, what are they? Was this service experience connected with anything in Scripture? Connected with anything in our faith? Has your understanding of Scripture, faithfulness, or your relationship with God been affected? If so, how?

After the youth have had an opportunity to reflect on their thoughts, share in small groups, and do some large group reflection with you, invite them to journal their own thoughts and prayers. They may have a journal just for reflective prayers following service opportunities. Conclude this prayer time with a group prayer: your prayer, their prayers of thanks, prayers about what they have learned, or prayers for the needs of the people they served and/or worked with in this experience.

Rebus prayer

A rebus story or poem is a combination of words and pictures. Invite your children/youth to create a rebus prayer. One way of doing this is to have within your meeting place a box that contains many diverse pictures. Invite each child/youth to choose seven of them (or any number you choose). Have them weave these pictures into a creative rebus prayer.

Rewrite prayers

Use some of our scriptural prayers or the Church's formal prayers, inviting the children/youth to rewrite them in their own words, with today's images and today's events. You might do this with Psalm 23, the Benedictus, the Our Father, or the Hail Mary.

Rites of forgiveness

Conversion is not a once-in-a-lifetime moment but a continuous, ongoing, lifelong process that brings us ever closer to the holiness and love of God.

One of the ways we grow in our journey of conversion is through prayerful rituals of forgiveness. The Church's Rite of Penance provides three sacramental Rites of Penance and a non-sacramental Penitential Service. This non-sacramental service, of course, does not need to be led by a priest.

For the children/youth, these services can be significant times of reflecting on their gifts and ways/places for growth as well as gratitude and celebration of God's forgiveness. Advent and Lent are ideal times for these rites, as well as other times of the year.

Pray with our rituals and gestures

Our faith abounds with rituals and gestures, within our liturgy and sacramental system, within the seasons of the liturgical year. Reverently use them during the prayer of your learning community. It will help prayer come more alive for them, as well as giving them a more tactile way of understanding and appreciating the symbols and rituals used during parish prayer.

Renew baptismal promises; use holy water; slowly pray the Sign of the Cross; share the Sign of Peace; bless with oil; share bread together; reverently pass around a cross; bless yourselves and one another; make the Sign of the Cross on your foreheads, lips, and hearts before hearing the gospel; use laying on of hands; use incense; make use of the Advent wreath, and palm branches during Holy Week; etc.

Round the world prayer

Provide your children/youth with experiences of prayer traditions from around the world. For example, Muslims stop five times a day to pray. Eastern religions put emphasis on breathing and body posture. The psalm prayers of the Hebrew people are chanted.

Encourage them to research the various prayer forms and practices of other traditions—Native American, Buddhist, Hindu, Jewish, and Islamic.

S s

Cardinal John Dearden, former archbishop of Detroit, once spoke of prayer at a liturgy for deceased priests of the archdiocese. "At death, we go to meet the Lord. What a difference there will be between meeting him as close friend to continue a conversation that has been carried on each day for years and years, or meeting him as someone a bit less familiar, someone to whom we are going to have to say some things for the first time."

▶ Does my prayer life resemble a close friendship with God?

▶ What topics of conversation do God and I talk about?

If we could all hear one another's prayers, God might be relieved of some of his burdens. • ASHLEIGH BRILLIANT

▶ Has your prayer ever moved you to do or be something for the person (situation) for which you're praying?

▶ Do our prayers ever tell God how to take care of the world?

Samaritan prayers

Form prayer teams of three or four people, asking each team to brainstorm one place in your community where people are in need—a hospital, a homeless shelter, a literacy center, a food pantry, etc. Have each team read James 2:14–26. Invite the teams to do as much research as they can to find out about the work of these places.

Then, have them brainstorm things they could do to be involved with the work, as well as things they could suggest to the parish that other parish members could do to be of assistance.

Invite them then to write prayers for the people, as well as for the parish efforts of outreach—prayers that can be published in your Sunday church bulletin to keep the needs and your efforts in prayerful perspective.

Praying with Scripture

Scripture pervades so much of what we do in our faith formation sessions. Thus, there are many ways that our prayer can flow from Scripture. Here are a few possibilities:

Invite one youth to proclaim the Scripture passage. After a moment for quiet reflection, invite them to share with each other: "What do you *see* in this Scripture passage? What image or picture comes to your mind?"

After everyone who wishes to has had a chance to share their thoughts, invite another youth to read the passage a second time. Following this reading, invite them to answer the question, "What did you *hear* in this Scripture passage? What word or phrase stood out more clearly—for you—than the others?"

Following this sharing, invite a third person to read the passage again. Invite your group: "Connect what you *heard* with what you *saw* in this Scripture passage. What do you need to *do* to follow Jesus better right now? How can you connect this Scripture to your daily life?"

You might also invite sharing on what this passage means to them as a group, not only to them as individuals.

After the sharing has ended, the prayer time can conclude with intercessions and the Our Father.

Some other ways to use Scripture in prayer:

- After hearing the Word proclaimed, take time for each person to reflect and then share with others their reflections: What did Jesus want me to hear today in this reading?

- Display a short verse from Scripture. Invite the children/ youth to sit in silence and listen as you reverently read (and perhaps re-read) the verse. When they are ready, they can begin a letter to Jesus in their journals about whatever thoughts spring to their minds from this Scripture passage.

- As has been mentioned previously, personalize a Scripture passage. See yourself in the boat with the apostles and Jesus during the raging storm. Walk on water with Peter. Discover the empty tomb with Mary Magdalene. How would you feel? What would you say? What would you do?

Sculpting prayer

Prayer can be expressed through one's hands and fingers working modeling clay, Play-doh, or aluminum foil. Not only is the process of modeling a potentially prayerful experience, but the finished work may remain as a reminder and facilitator of prayer.

One method is to suggest to the children/youth that the purpose of the prayer is not to create "an object" as they would in an art class. Explore a Scripture passage, such as Jesus' call to us to be the salt of the earth and the light of the world. After reflecting and discussing together what that might mean in their lives, invite your young learners to close their eyes and work with the clay in their hands for several minutes. Talk with God, listen to God—working the clay, but not consciously "making" anything.

After several minutes, invite them to close their quiet prayer and to reverently look at the clay or foil in their hands. Look at it from all directions. What does it say to you? What meaning does it have for you? What meaning does it have for your life right now?

Prayer of the secret word

We can learn much from the reverent spirituality and prayer of the Native Americans. One Native American prayer is the prayer of the secret word. At the beginning of the day (or week), Native Americans listen in silence for their secret word. In silent prayer, they quiet their bodies and minds. After welcoming the Holy Spirit into their lives, they listen for the word that is meant to guide their life at this particular moment.

Once they have heard the word, they take it into their hearts in prayer, and they take it to their feet because, knowing it is God's Word, they are going to walk it all day (all week) in all that they do.

Praying with the senses

We are embodied people; that is the miraculous way God created us. Therefore, God doesn't expect us to pray with just words, but also to use our senses. It is why the Church, in her wisdom, uses incense, touch, oil, blessings, processions, bows, etc.

Saint Ignatius of Loyola encourages the use of the senses in his *Spiritual Exercises*. Ignatius believed the whole person could and should enter into prayer. He promoted using the senses, the memory, and the imagination to project oneself into a gospel passage.

Thus, as a catechist, lead your learners through prayers such as this: During the miraculous catch of fish after the resurrection, Jesus is on the beach cooking breakfast for his disciples on a charcoal fire.

- What does the beach look like?

- How cold is the water?

- What is the smell of grilled fish and bread?

- How loud are the waves?

- Imagine yourself as one of the disciples, wet from the spray coming over the side of the boat, relieved and amazed at the catch of the fish, suddenly realizing that the stranger on the beach is Jesus. How then do you go to Jesus?

- What would you say to him?

- What do you hear?

Sign of the Cross

The Sign of the Cross is probably the most commonly used prayer of Christians, and most likely the first prayer we learned as children. Despite its simplicity, the Sign of the Cross is an ancient prayer rich in meaning. References to it appear in writings dating back to 240 AD, and it is believed that it was in use during the earliest days of Christianity.

The Sign of the Cross is primarily a blessing. We use it to ask God's blessing on us.

When we make the Sign of the Cross, we are also expressing our belief in God and the Trinity. Through it, we remind ourselves of God's love for us, of Jesus' commitment to a way of life he came to teach us and share with us, and of the presence of the Holy Spirit within us.

Each time we pray it, it is a renewal of our baptism; we say again, in effect, "I died with Christ and rose to new life." The sign links us to the Body of Christ, and with Christ as the head.

Because of our baptism, the Sign of the Cross is a mark of discipleship. We are recommitting ourselves to be Jesus' followers, to be Jesus in our world.

Because of such profound meanings, this simple — but weighty — prayer cannot be prayed quickly, without thinking. Therefore, at times, invite your learners to pray the Sign of Cross very deliberately, focusing their attention on the words and actions. You might suggest or review one of the meanings before praying. Sometimes, your prayer time itself might only consist of praying the Sign of the Cross — with a reflective time upon the words and ritual.

Signing of the Senses

During the Rite of Acceptance into the Catechumenate (in the *Rite of Christian Initiation of Adults* [RCIA]), one of the rituals is the Signing of the Senses (RCIA, #54–56). The format of this ritual can be adapted to use with our children and youth.

One adaptation would be to gather for prayer at the beginning of the year, inviting the parents to join you for the first or last twenty minutes of your session. They then would sign their child/youth with the Sign of the Cross as each prayer is prayed: e.g., "Receive the Sign of the Cross on your lips. May you always speak with wisdom, with concern for others, and truth."

Pray about the signs of the times

The Pastoral Constitution on the Church in the Modern World (*Gaudium et Spes*) from the Second Vatican Council said, "Hence this Second Vatican Council, having probed more profoundly into the mystery of the Church, now addresses itself without hesitation, not only to the sons (and daughters) of the Church and to all who invoke the name of Christ, but to the whole of humanity....To carry out such a task, the Church has always had the duty of scrutinizing the signs of the times and of interpreting them in the light of the gospel" (#2, 4).

The signs of the times, what is happening in the everyday world, in the everyday lives of each and every person, is important to God and to the Church. God asks that it be important to us.

To pray about the signs of the times is to open our hearts, to widen our hearts, to see as God sees. We lose our sense of "we and they" or "them and us" or "me and mine." Our hearts open to take in the whole world.

In our prayer with our young learners, we can, we need to, gently lead them to read the signs of the times, seeing those signs through God's eyes. They are the future leaders of the world and the Church. They need to lead as prayerful prophets.

Prayer of silence

Silence and solitude are at the core of a life of prayer. In our noisy, busy world, there isn't much time for silence unless we make it. Provide moments of quiet within prayer times, giving opportunities for meditation, and you will find children/youth asking for more.

When possible, take opportunities to leave all electronic devices behind and walk the children/youth into a quiet, natural place near your meeting place or chapel or church; ask them to stop, sit, listen, reflect. Then bring them back and ask them about the time, their feelings, their experiences.

Or just walk in silence. It doesn't have to be a specific place. Just go for a short walk; it can even be within the building. Simply invite them to walk in silence. Rest in God.

A Scripture passage that calls us to silence and solitude comes from the psalms: "Be still and know that I am God" (46:11). A helpful, quieting meditation is to take that short call and meditate on it, slowly dropping one word at a time from the end of the sentence, thus reflecting on the new statement:

Be still and know that I am

Be still and know that I

Be still and know that

Be still and know

Be still and

Be still

Be

Silent circle prayer

Invite your children to gather in a circle, asking them to think of things for which they are thankful. Begin the prayer by saying, "Loving God, who cares for us so much, we are thankful for so many things." Then have each child pantomime one thing he/she is grateful for.

After all have reverently finished, lead the group in prayerfully singing a song of thanks.

Stations of the Cross

The Stations of the Cross has long been a popular devotion used by individuals or groups who wish through prayer and reflection to follow Jesus on his way to Calvary.

The devotion originated in the late fourth century when pilgrims flocked to the Holy Land from all parts of the world to visit the land of Jesus. Heading the list of places they visited was the Church of the Holy Sepulcher, which had been built by the Emperor Constantine about 335 AD atop Calvary and the tomb of Jesus. Promotion of the devotion to the Stations began in earnest with the Franciscans, who were given custody of the Holy Places in the Holy Land in the 1300s.

In recent years some variations have been introduced into the traditional devotion. One is the addition of a fifteenth station—the Resurrection of Jesus. Another is a series of scriptural stations, which begins with the Agony of Jesus in Gethsemane and omits some of the traditional non-scriptural stations in favor of incidents mentioned in the gospels. Pope John Paul II celebrated a series of scriptural stations on Good Friday in 1991, and again in 1994, in the Colosseum at Rome.

There are many ways your children/youth can pray this devotion, especially during the lenten season:

- Pray this prayer using one of the many booklets available today for children or youth.

- Invite them to write their own prayers and meditations for the Stations.

- Have the children/youth write a modern-day version of the Stations of the Cross. Where are people experiencing suffering, betrayal, etc., today?

Stations of the Resurrection

Rooted in an ancient tradition, Christians are rediscovering the Stations of the Resurrection (the *Via Lucis*, the way of light) that parallel the Stations of the Cross (the *Via Crucis*).

The Stations of Light highlight the resurrection appearances and faith encounters with the Risen Lord from all four gospels:

1. Jesus Rises from the Dead

2. The Disciples Discover the Empty Tomb

3. The Risen Lord Appears to Mary Magdalene, Apostle to the Apostles

4. The Risen Lord Appears on the Road to Emmaus

5. The Risen Lord is Recognized in the Breaking of the Bread

6. The Risen Lord Appears to the Community of Disciples

7. The Risen Lord Breathes Peace and Gives the Power to Forgive

8. The Risen Lord Strengthens the Faith of Thomas

9. The Risen Lord Eats with the Disciples on the Shores of Tiberias

10. The Risen Lord Forgives Peter and Entrusts Him to Tend and Feed His Sheep

11. The Risen Lord Sends the Disciples into the World

12. The Risen Lord Ascends into Heaven

13. Mary and the Disciples Keep Vigil in the Upper Room for the Spirit's Advent

14. The Risen Lord Sends the Holy Spirit

Several meditations and services for the Stations of the Resurrection can be found on the Internet. Your children/youth could work in groups to create prayers and paintings to depict each station, forming a prayer service for all fourteen Stations.

Sunday's psalm refrain

Often we pay attention to the three Sunday readings (we should); but do we forget about the Responsorial Psalm that we sing each weekend, especially the refrain from the psalm? The psalms are powerful prayers of our heritage. The refrains capture the emotions of praise, trust, and dependence upon God, such as:

- We are his people, the sheep of his flock.

- The Lord is kind and merciful.

- Remember, O Lord, your faithfulness and love.

- We praise you, O God, for all your works are wonderful.

- All the ends of the earth have seen the saving power of God.

- Be with me, Lord, when I am in trouble.

- Lord, you have the words of everlasting life.

The refrain from Sunday's psalm does not have to end on Sunday. Use that refrain as a prayer phrase to be sung or prayed frequently by your group throughout the week. Suggest that it become a family prayer throughout the week; family members could pledge to pray it at a certain time each day (e.g., noon) even though they might be apart.

T t

> ▶ How often are your prayers prayers of thanks?
>
> ▶ For what do you give thanks? Might there be other things for which to give thanks?
>
> ▶ How often do you pray prayers of thanks in your catechetical setting?
>
> ▶ In what ways do you suggest ideas for prayers of thanks for your children's/youth's families at home?

Thanksgiving prayers

To be thanks-givers is to know who we are. The prayer of thanks is profound, because in it we recognize that "Every good gift, every genuine benefit comes from above, descending from the Father of the heavenly luminaries, who cannot change and who is never shadowed over" (James 1:17). To lead children/youth to a relationship with God based on such trust and gratitude is one of the most awe-inspiring privileges we have.

A few methods for prayers of thanksgiving are:

- Help your young people create a small booklet that they can use at home each evening to reflect upon their day in gratitude. Their prayer of thanks for the day can have four parts:

  > Ever-present God, I thank you for the good things of today: for the good people I was with _____;
  >
  > for the good times I had _____;
  >
  > for the good things that happened to me _____;
  >
  > and for the good things I was able to do for someone else _____.

- A brightly decorated box or jar with the word "Thanks" can be placed in your group's prayer space. Next to the box place a supply of pencils and 3 x 5 cards. Invite the children/youth to jot down their prayers of thanks whenever they have time and place them in the box or jar. A jar that is growing with more and more contributions is a visible reminder of the countless things for which to give thanks. Periodically, this box or jar can be opened and the prayers used as part of the group's prayer time.

- Purchase or make a beautiful journal for your group. Periodically, as a group, brainstorm things for which to say "thank you." Have various people take turns writing or drawing them in your group journal. You can also invite the children/youth to add to the journal at any time on their own.

- A journal of thanks can be used in many ways, not only as a remembrance of each day's big and little events. It can coincide with specific lesson themes. During a unit on the gift of forgiveness, children can be encouraged to recall and write about the times in their lives when they have experienced the acceptance and forgiveness of others. A creation theme of study might help young people to reflect on the smallest things in God's world, or the brightest things.

- Sometimes, putting ourselves in the place of another gives us a new outlook and deepens our awareness of gratitude for life. In conjunction with the theme of the lesson, invite your children and youth to pretend they are a specific person in Scripture, a person currently in the news, an animal, etc., and write a prayer of thanks from his or her viewpoint.

Prayer in three words

One of the television networks today has a segment on Saturday mornings titled "The Week in Three Words." Viewers are invited to send in a short video of themselves (their family, friends, coworkers, etc.) with a synopsis or a highlight of their week in three words.

Use this creative method to invite your learners to write a short prayer (and leave the rest of prayer time for listening to God). The "theme" of the prayer can be changed for different occasions and settings, such as:

- a prayer of thanks
- a prayer of peace
- a prayer about this past week
- a prayer for a close friend
- a prayer for the world
- a prayer of sorrow
- a prayer for yourself

Trading cards

Design, copy, and cut apart two "prayer trading cards" for each child/youth in the group. While designing the cards, place these categories on the back of each card: your name, your dream for God's world, your prayer request.

As you give each learner two cards, invite them to draw a picture of themselves on the front of each card. Have them autograph each card, filling out their dreams and what one of their prayer needs is at the present time.

After reading and reflecting on Ephesians 6:18, invite your learners to walk around the learning space and trade cards with each other. They need to trade cards with at least three different people (until the time is up—about one minute). As they trade, they know that they will be praying for the people whose cards they end up with.

Encourage the children/youth to let each other know they have their cards and they will be praying for them. Suggest to them that they place the cards somewhere at home where they'll see them every day, remembering to pray. After about three to four weeks, you can do the process again so that they receive more "trading cards," and new people to remember in prayer.

Turn-around prayers

A turn-around prayer is a sentence prayer in which the first part of the sentence acknowledges a blessing that children/youth might enjoy and the second part recognizes that there are some who do not share in that blessing. The simple steps:

1. Invite your learners to make a list of all the blessings they enjoy from God.

2. Opposite each idea on the list, describe what life is like for people who do not share in that blessing.

3. Choose one of these ideas and its opposite, and use it to write a turn-around prayer. The format of the prayer can be: When I (state blessing), O God, help me to (remember those who don't share in the blessing). For example: When my friend and I have fun outside together, O God, help me to think about those right now who are lonely and have no friends.

Twenty-third psalm

Probably no other psalm is as familiar to people as the Twenty-Third Psalm, "The Lord is my Shepherd." Various translations and numerous musical adaptations are available. Yet, as we know, the symbols, language, and assumptions of Old Testament times are likely to be different from those of today, even though the core meaning remains the same.

With older learners, a prayerful learning experience can occur in the rewriting of this psalm in today's language and images.

U u

A little boy was praying intently before he went to bed: "Dear God, please take care of my daddy and my mommy and my sister and my brother and my doggy and me. Oh, please take care of yourself, God. If anything happens to you, we're gonna be in a big mess."

► Am I that convinced of my dependence on God?

► As a catechist, how can I help my children/youth become more filled with trust, with wonder at God's care for them?

Unfinished prayer

Suggest an incomplete prayer to the children/youth, inviting them to finish it based on their current needs and feelings. These can be done individually and then shared, or the whole group can work together on a prayer.

For example, "God, you are____. Help us to _____. We love you because _____."

V v

> *God understands our prayers even when we can't find the words to say them…* • ANONYMOUS
>
> ▶ What do you do in times when no words will come?
>
> ▶ How would you explain these times to your children/youth?

Video and media clips

Consider using video and media clips as prayer starters, to help children/youth focus their thoughts for prayer. "The Circle of Life" sequence from the Disney movie *The Lion King* could be a reflective way to begin a prayer focused on the wonders of creation and the goodness of our God.

The YouTube video "Father's Love Letter" is a letter from God to "My Child." It is taken from Scripture and accompanied by visuals. When watching the video, the children/youth can each be asked to write down one line that touches them. When it is over, they can reflect for a minute in silence, followed by sharing their reflections.

They can then be given a copy of the "letter." After reading it over, they are asked to underline a phrase, word, or sentence that touches them. It may be the same or a different phrase from the

132

one chosen before. Another opportunity for sharing can follow this reflection.

As you always seek to pray in solidarity with those in your community, your nation, and throughout the world who need prayer and support, you can even use clips from news shows as a prelude to, or integral to, prayer times.

Visio divina

Visio divina is a contemplative practice of praying the Scriptures while viewing images or other media. The practice of visio divina has three parts: a reading of Scripture, viewing the art/media, and responding as individuals or in small groups. Visio divina (divine seeing) has its roots in the ancient practice of lectio divina (divine reading).

As we look through Scripture, images have been an important part of God's way of communicating with us throughout history. Ezekiel's vision of dry bones and Peter's vision on the rooftop in Acts 10 are two instances of how images and prayer are vitally connected.

As our culture is becoming more and more visually oriented—especially for young people—an intentional way of praying with images is needed now more than ever. Visio divina invites us to see at a more contemplative pace. It invites us to *see* all there is to see. It invites us to see deeply. It invites us to be seen, addressed, surprised, and transformed by God, who is never limited or tied to any image, but speaks through them.

After reading the Scripture, invite your young learners to slowly look and notice the image, taking time to let their feelings and thoughts come as they take in the forms, figures, colors, lines, textures, and shapes. What does it look like, or remind them of? What do they find themselves drawn to? What do they like and not like? What are their feelings? Give time to explore the art/media and their responses, as well as sharing responses with one another. It can be fascinating. The variety of responses to art/media can be even more vast than to the written word.

A large variety, of course, of art and media can be used to evoke prayerful responses. Liturgical Press is creating a series called *Seeing the Word* (www.seeingtheword.org). The full series is designed for adults, but as the site indicates, the images themselves have been prayerfully used with all ages, beginning with first-graders.

Another site, which was created for adults but may be helpful background and inspiration for you, is PrayerWindows (www.prayerwindows.com) by Bob Gilroy, SJ, in which he uses paintings to display a way to pray in a creative manner.

Visualizing prayers

Our imaginations are a gift from God, one that can be used in prayer. Many experts tell us that positive thinking influences our lives, and Scripture says the same: "As face mirrors face in water, so the heart reflects the person" (Proverbs 27:19).

Encourage your children/youth to use the gift of imagination in prayer. When they are praying for someone to be healed, encourage them to picture that person as peace-filled. In prayers of reconciliation, they can imagine the resolution of the conflict, the friendship renewed, and God's peace surrounding everyone.

W w

> *Granting that we are always in the presence of God, yet it seems to me that those who pray are in God's presence in a very different sense; for they, as it were, see that God is looking upon them.* • SAINT TERESA OF AVILA

- ▶ How does this make you feel—that God is looking upon you?
- ▶ Which type of prayer intensifies your awareness of God's presence?

> *All real prayer must begin in wonder.* • TAD DUNNE, SJ

- ▶ What causes you to wonder?
- ▶ How do you lead your children/youth to wonder?

Walk and pray

Take a walk through the building where you meet, through your church, or through the outside grounds, giving the children/youth a chance to offer prayers at various spots along the way. For instance: By the pews: "We pray that many people will learn about you today." Near the parish offices: "Thank you, Loving

God, for the people who minister in our parish, who help our community grow closer together and closer to you so we can make the world a better place." By a tree or garden: "Creator God, we are a part of the vastness of your magnificent creation. We promise to care for each and every marvel, always finding new ways to respect what you have given."

Walking prayer

The wonderful spiritual writer and religious educator Sr. José Hobday used to tell this story of when she was a little girl: One of her favorite ways of praying was to take prayer walks, walking in nature, enraptured with her God, and lost in prayer. Once when she left the house on one of her walks into God's creation to be with God, her somewhat-skeptical father turned to her mother, saying, "Come on now, how do you really know that when she goes off like this, she's praying?"

Her wise mother simply replied, "How do you know she's not?"

At times, invite your children/youth outside for a prayer walk, saying, "We won't talk, won't use words for our prayer today. Just walk slowly and reverently. Look, listen. Think about how God loves you. Thank God for whatever comes to your mind."

When you return to your place, you may want to share reflections on what it was like for the children/youth. One of the ramifications of this experience is that it "teaches" our young people that prayer can happen and God can be worshiped any where, any time.

What's in a name?

This activity is a prelude to, a preparation for, prayer. It's important, for how we think about God impacts our prayer immensely!

At times, we don't stop to think about the meaning of names, and "God" might be used without reflection. Ask the children/ youth to play this game with you for a certain number of weeks. No one will use the word "God" unless he/she uses an adjective with it (e.g., Gracious God) or a longer phrase that describes God (e.g., God who loves us).

This can help to personalize their concept of God and make praying more personal.

Wheel of prayer

Use a prayer wheel on your prayer bulletin board. Some weeks, the wheel can designate different prayers for the different days of the week (acts of faith on Monday, acts of love on Tuesday, etc.).

For other weeks, the wheel can indicate different intentions for different days of the week (Monday: for people who are lonely; Tuesday: for people throughout the world who are hungry; etc.).

Witness shoes

Have an assortment of shoes (or pictures of shoes, or PowerPoint of shoe pictures), for example: gym shoes, dress shoes, soccer shoes, ballet slippers, sandals, inline skates, etc. Each child/youth chooses a shoe and asks God's help in following Jesus where the shoe might be worn. "Dear God, help me to always remember to take turns on the playground." "Help me to remember to listen to my coach during the soccer game."

Wonder prayer

Read the story of creation (Genesis 1:1–31; 2:4-24), or a psalm that thanks God for the beauty of the earth (Psalms 8, 33, 98, 100, 104, 128, 148, 150). With song, dance, poetry, or some other form of art, invite your young learners to compose a prayer that expresses their thanks for the wonders of creation.

X x Y y Z z

During family meal prayers, Dad ended grace one night with "Amen."

One of his children, paying very close attention that evening, asked what it meant.

Before he or his wife could respond, their five-year-old answered, "It means 'send.'"

Even though we have probably heard many explanations of the word "Amen," this humorous, insightful story, from a young child, invites us to another reflection about our trust in God.

► Do I hand over my prayers to God in simplicity and trust?

► Do I really know — and feel — that God is interested and listening to all the concerns of my everyday life?

► As a catechist, am I giving enough time for prayer so that the children/youth develop an integrated attitude of prayer that is trusting, confident, and faith-filled?

In prayer, come empty, do nothing.

• ST. JOHN OF THE CROSS

► Is it difficult for you to do nothing in prayer?

► What do you do to "come empty" to prayer?

X-Y-Z prayer

Give each child/youth a different letter of the alphabet, and invite them to draw or paint pictures of things that begin with that letter.

Gather for prayer in your prayer space and begin, "Most loving God, you have given us so many diverse, distinctive things, each one showing your love for us. Now, one by one, we thank you for some of these...."

Each child/youth then shows his/her picture, praying a prayer of thanks.

Prayer of yes

Invite children/youth to incorporate into their prayer an attitude like that of Mary, so their attitude and their life may always be a yes to God.